I0233682

A CUP OF DAILY WISDOM FOR YOUR MARRIAGE

A Marriage Devotional

Loretta A. Pittman

Copyright © 2014 by Scriptures Publishing

Scriptures Publishing

639 Saint Anthony Lane,

Upper Darby Pa, 19082

All rights reserved.

ISBN-13: 978-0-692-28844-3
ISBN-10: 0692288449
Library of Congress Control Number: 2014917459

DEDICATION

I dedicate this book to our Lord and Savor for this assignment in helping Me learn to be submissive to my husband and so marriages all over the world can be delivered and healed. I thank you lord for the lessons and the wisdom that was put forth to bring about this book. Lord you are everything to me and I am nothing without your Holy Spirit.

I also want to thank my husband William K. Pittman, who was the true inspiration for this book without you babe I wouldn't have been able to get through this process. I love you with all my heart.

I also want to thank everyone who contributed their testimony for the success of this book. Pastor Marvin and Deborah Jackson of (The River of Life Christian Center) located in Orlando FL,

Pastor DeCarlo & Marion Sabedra of (Abundant Life Family Worship Center) located in Orlando FL,
Lee and Felissa Gully of Lawrenceville Ga,
Thomas and Patricia Williams of (Miracle House of Healing) located in Sanford FL, and Herb & Sharon Lee of Philadelphia Pa. Thanks again so much you all are the best!

I also would like to dedicate this book to my grown children Rebbie, DeAndre, Jamal, Takiyah and our grandchildren Seven, Messiah, Serenity, Wisdom and future grand
children your Father/Grandfather, and I love you all to pieces may God continue to bless you all in your process in life. We also would like to thank all our friends and family we love you all.

A Cup of Daily Wisdom for Your Marriage

CONTENTS

Forward:

A Cup of Daily Wisdom for Your Marriage is a must read!!!!

If you need wisdom in your marriage, then this book will help you achieve that. I have seen the growth in our marriage over the years because of wisdom. God has taken our marriage to the next level because of the principles he has taught us in this book. My wife is now my best friend, confidant and love of my life. You too can achieve a deeper love for your spouse.
Thank You baby I'm so proud of you.

Bishop William K. Pittman

Founder Of
New Covenant of Faith Int'l Ministries

ACKNOWLEDGMENTS

God is the author of marriage, and he gave us marriage to keep us from sin and to bare Godly offspring. Marriage is formed for one man, and one woman. Marriage was not designed for divorce, cheating or abuse.
God showed me in a dream a collection of wedding rings in a corner and then he showed me couples were taking off their wedding rings and throwing them in the pile, right then God spoke to me and said Loretta they don't understand that marriage is a Covenant before me and it's Important!

Wedding vows are not just words we say or words on a piece of paper. When we enter a marriage, we enter a covenant with God and our spouse just like God is married to the church. It is God's design, and we enter it before him, therefore it's his covenant that we come into an agreement with. There are so many people just throwing marriage away not knowing how important it is to God.

When we love, serve, follow and give our lives to God we now have entered a covenant marriage relationship with him. In a marriage, you vow to love your spouse and live with them until death does you part. It's the same when we give our lives to Christ they go hand in hand. We need marriage wisdom to help us stay married and to help us keep our covenant marriage agreement with God and before God.

A Cup of Daily Wisdom for Your Marriage

LORETTA'S STORY

It all started one day when my grandmother came to our home in Philadelphia for a visit and this handsome young guy arrived with her to drop her off at our house. My sister Tina and I heard voices while we, were upstairs talking and doing our hair so we came down the stairs to see who was there and that's when I saw William for the first time. I told my sister "that's my husband" and she said how do you know, and I told her I don't know but my spirit says that is him.

Isaiah 55:11 says: **So, shall my word be that goes out from my mouth; it shall not return to me empty, but it shall accomplish that which I purpose, and shall succeed in the thing for which I sent it.**

I was born in Cape May New Jersey on August eleventh nineteen sixty-nine and I grew up in Wildwood New Jersey. That was a happy time in my life as a child. It was just me, my mom, and my sister Tina at that time and we had so much fun as kids living in Wildwood near the beach. Our mother was a single mom who was always involved in our schooling, she would keep us busy taking swimming lessons and going to summer camp it was such an awesome time as a kid.

Proverbs 22:6 Train up a child in the way he should go, and when he is old he will not depart from it

I just loved going to the beach and just having fun in the sand. My sister Tina and I was always together I pretty much taught her everything from how to tie her shoes to how to get dressed it was just such a fun time growing up. My mother was a loving person who always took in family members back in those days who would lose their jobs or who just needed some help and sometimes that meant her brothers. Well this one brother of her's uncle Nate use to always stay with us and for some odd reason my mom would make him sleep in the bed with my sister and I and that's where my first sexual abuse experience happened.

Matthew 18:6 but whoever causes one of these little ones who believe in me to sin, it would be better for him to have a great millstone fastened around his neck and to be drowned in the depth of the sea.

I was about seven or eight years old when one night I woke up to uncle Nate performing what I now know was oral sex on me. I was so shocked, I didn't understand what was happening to me. I was scared, because I didn't know what sex was at that age. I was too scared to let my mother know what was happening for the fear that she wouldn't believe me. This went on several more times until one-night uncle Nate and his brother uncle Chuck went out and stole something from an ice cream store that was near us. Once the cops came looking for them my mother threw them out and that stopped my first experience with sexual abuse. I never spoke of it again until now writing this book.

Jeremiah 1:5 says: Before I formed you in the womb I knew you; Before you were born I sanctified you; I ordained you a prophet to the nations. When I was little I always knew there was a God I can remember talking to God as young as five years old. At that time, it was just my mom and I for three years until my sister Tina came. I would talk to God all the time especially when I was alone. I would always tell him what I wanted when I grew up and I would hear him talk back to me too that was so normal for me growing up.

As time went on still living in Wildwood my mother met a man named Glasgow Rex whom she had three more kids and then later married. My sister and I at first thought the world of him. It seemed like he truly loved my mom and that he loved us but as time would have it the real him would show up. More time went by and another baby sister came along, and we were so excited to have her. It was like having a new baby doll to look after we would dress her and comb her hair it was such a welcomed surprise. We would have so much fun as a family until we moved out of Wildwood to Philadelphia that's where life totally began to change.

Romans 12:2 says: Do not be conformed to this world, but be transformed by the renewal of your mind, that by testing you may discern what is the will of God, what is good and acceptable and perfect."

My mother and her husband moved us to Uber Street in North Philadelphia back in the late seventies and living in that house became a nightmare. We lived in the house with my grandfather, my uncle Chuck who was close to my age and my grandfather's girlfriend. We lived on the top floor and they lived on the bottom floor. My mom just changed after she got married. Her and husband started going out and drinking to point that they would come home yelling and fighting each other. My mother would get so mad at him that she would go and get a knife and start trying stab him. It was such an abusive and toxic situation. I was always left to watch my two sisters and I was so young myself I would be scared, and my sisters would be crying and screaming because of their fighting. We just really hated when they told us they were going out because we knew they would come home fighting with each other.

1 Peter 3:7 says: Likewise, husbands, live with your wives in an understanding way, showing honor to the woman as the weaker vessel, since they are heirs with you of the grace of life, so that your prayers may not be hindered.

The way they communicated shaped the way I would communicate with my husband in the beginning of my marriage, once I got married little did I know. I used to say to myself watching them that I would never have a marriage like theirs.

Proverbs 25:11 says: A word fitly spoken is like apples of gold in a setting of silver.

Like I told you earlier my mother was always taking in those who needed help and so a sister of hers came to live with us after she got old enough to move out on her own and that's when my step father started his sexual advances toward her. We had a set of bunk beds in our room and the way our room was made there were walls but no doors so if you were sleep and someone came over

4

if my mom bought them to the back of the house they could see you while you were sleeping.

One night my step father Glasgow came into our room while my aunt and I was sleeping on the top bunk and he began to pull up our night gowns and would just stand there looking at us like some sick creep. On this one night I caught him, and he looked me right in my face and hurried up and left our room. I told my aunt the next day and so we both made up our minds to take turns staying up to watch him and make sure he didn't do it again, but when we were so tired from keeping watch it was happening again and again. My aunt didn't want to tell my mother for fear that she would blame her. You see there was a history of that in our family. If you told a woman in this family that their man was coming on to you, they would immediately believe the man and blame you.

Galatians 6:5 For we are each responsible for our own conduct.

More time passed, and my mother and step father saved enough money for them to buy a house and they did. We were so glad when we moved from North Philadelphia to the suburbs of Germantown Pennsylvania. Our new home was located at five twenty-five east Walnut Lane and we just knew we had money. We had a room with a door a porch to sit on and nice neighbors with a yard to play in we truly loved our new neighborhood. But that didn't last long.

My aunt moved in with us and it seemed everything was going to be ok, but little did we know my step father would become very controlling. My aunt started dating and it seemed like my step father was jealous because he would always start an argument with my mother about my auntie and her dating life. My aunt dated her boyfriend for a while so when she got pregnant with her first child my step father got mad. I guess he felt she betrayed him by getting pregnant, so he found a way for my mother to get mad at her, so she would put her out. And that's what she did right after my aunt had her baby my mother told her she had to leave, and it was in the dead of winter with no place to go. It was the saddest time for us because we truly loved her, and we wanted to grow up with the baby.

Romans 8:28 - And we know that for those who love God all things work together for good, for those who are called according to his purpose.

It was dead of winter when my mother told her to leave like I said earlier but thank God for grandma who she went to live with. After her departure I was his next target he would be mean towards us and would start fights with my mother, so I would always be in trouble or on punishment. I couldn't have friends and don't even think about having a boyfriend it was just horrible growing up in that house.

Ephesians 1:11 - In him we have obtained an inheritance, having been predestined according to the

purpose of him who works all things according to the counsel of his will.

The abuse started when I was thirteen that's when my mother's husband crossed the line of step father to sexual predator. He started out looking at me with lust whenever my mother wasn't around which made me very uncomfortable and it made me hide my body. I would put on layers of clothes just, so my body wouldn't show and so he couldn't lust after it, but that only lasted a little while. Our bedroom my sisters and I was right down the hall from my mother's bedroom and my bed was right in front of the door, so he would be looking at me sleeping and when I would wake up I could see him watching me. I was so scared and disgusted I would just keep our door closed so he couldn't see in anymore.

My mother would work out of town in Atlantic City a lot to make ends meet and he would wake me up as soon as she would leave about 6am in the morning and he would beat me and punch me for it seemed like hours for no reason. Then one day he tried touching my breasts and he tried putting his mouth on my breast when I pushed him off me and I knew then he had crossed the line. I couldn't tell my mother because he said to me he would kill us if I did and I also feared she wouldn't believe me, so I began acting out and running away. I ran away to my Aunt Nadine's house and I told her what was happening to me so, she got on the phone with my mother and told her what was happening, and my mother didn't believe me just like I feared she would.

Psalm 27:10 says: For my father and my mother have forsaken me, but the Lord will take me in.

That is the most devastating thing in a child's life when something is happening to them and they are not believed. That situation shaped my relationship with my mother I felt distant from her and I cleaved more to my aunt Nadine and my grandmother who also believed me.

John 14:1 says: "Let not your hearts be troubled. Believe in God; believe also in me.

As Time went on another one of my mother's sisters moved in and by this time my other two siblings were already here. My mother's baby sister moved in and we had so much fun with her as well. I was especially glad she moved in because now his attention was on her and not me. My mother started working in Atlantic City again and leaving us home with my aunt and my step father whenever he would come home because he was the type of man who was always leaving home and you didn't know where he was or when he was coming back. sometimes it would be weeks or maybe a month and my mother would always take him back.

Hebrews 13:4 says: Let marriage be held in honor among all, and let the marriage bed be undefiled, for God will judge the sexually immoral and adulterous.

As soon as my mother's back was turned he started an affair with her baby sister. They were sleeping together which was fine by me if he wasn't touching me. Late one night my mother caught him coming out of her baby sister's room and she accused her sister and not him of doing something wrong. Even though she saw him creeping out of her baby sister's room she told her baby sister she had to move out. I was so sad because I knew his attention would be back on me.

1 Corinthians 6:18-20 Flee from sexual immorality. Every other sin a person commits is outside the body, but the sexually immoral person sins against his own body. Or do you not know that your body is a temple of the Holy Spirit within you, whom you have from God? You are not your own, for you were bought with a price. So, glorify God in your body.

As I told you earlier the women in my family would believe their man before they would believe you. After my mother didn't believe me and didn't believe her baby sister she now had to leave because of this man. That situation changed me to the point that I began to look for love and safety in all the wrong places.

My mother moved her younger brother uncle Chuck in with us and we were so happy because this was the uncle I told you about earlier that was close to my age and we were so close. We grew up together on Uber Street in the same house. It was always me, uncle Chuck and my sister Tina together wherever you would see us. One day we were home alone when uncle Chuck came on to me and tried to have sex with me but I was still a virgin then and so it didn't happen. He tried to penetrate me but couldn't, so he stopped, and got off me and I never spoke about it no more until now.

I truly loved uncle Chuck and because of that I was taken advantage of. I now know he was also a predator and I believe he was grooming me for that moment. After that incident I became promiscuous and I met a boy my same age fifteen at that time at school and on my first time having sex I ended up pregnant by him and afraid.

2Timothy 2:22 So flee youthful passions and pursue righteousness, faith, love, and peace, along with those who call on the Lord from a pure heart.

My mother ended up losing our home, so we relocated to Atlantic City New jersey and that ended the abuse again for a while for me. Once we moved to New Jersey I realized my body was changing and I had not seen my period and I was gaining weight. I didn't really know what it was to be pregnant, but I would feel something moving around in my belly. I did notice that my stomach was getting bigger, but I truly didn't know. By the time my mother took me to the doctor's I found out I was eight months pregnant. My mother never talked to us about sex and boys she let the child molester my step father give us his rendition of sex before I ended up pregnant, which consisted of the birds and bees. I was so confused I didn't have a clue what he was talking about.

On October twenty seventh nineteen eighty-four I had a beautiful seven-pound six-ounce baby daughter named Rebbie Violamae Wright that I was so proud to have. You see my mother didn't get mad at me for getting pregnant because she had me at that same age. I found out later that my mother got involved with my grandmother's boyfriend at that time and got pregnant with me. I believe my father molested her because she was only fourteen years old when she got pregnant with me and my father was already in his thirties or forties. You would think that she would have protected her daughters better from molestation knowing it happened to her, but I guess she was in denial. We ended up moving back to Philadelphia after my daughter was born and things still was not good. My step father started his old tricks again but this time he just kept looking at me with lust he never tried touching me again but just having to put up with the looks of lust was just as bad.

Luke 17:2 - It were better for him that a millstone were hanged about his neck, and he cast into the sea, than that he should offend one of these little ones.

In the summer of nineteen eighty-five I made up my mind to visit my grandmother for the summer and that's when I decided to leave all relationships alone and just focus on my daughter. Her father kept denying he was her father and that sealed it for me I didn't want no more relationships I just wanted it to be my daughter and I, but little did I know God had another plan. I visited my grandmother for the summer when I finally got to meet that handsome guy that bought my grandmother to our home in Philadelphia and his name was William, but they called him by his middle name Kelly.

I found out that William's mother and my grandmother were best friends working in the same restaurant in Atlantic City New Jersey back in the day. My grandmother saw my husband grow up, so she knew he was a good man.

My grandmother was working at the casino at the time I visited her, and we were on our way one day that summer to pick her up from work. That's when my aunt and my grandmother's friend, who was driving, seen William. He pulled up to the car yelling at my grandmother's boyfriend. They were yelling about who would get to the job faster and then they proceeded to race each other down the street to pick her up.

When we arrived, William got out of his car and got into the back seat of our car where my daughter and I was sitting. He greeted me with a warm smile and then proceeded to talk to my aunt and my grandmother's boyfriend. Suddenly, my aunt introduced us, and we exchanged names and then he asked me, "How old was the baby?"

I said, "She's eight-months old." Then he asked how old I was, and I told him that I was fifteen going on sixteen. He was like, "Oh I thought you were eighteen."
And I said "No, but I'll be eighteen if you want me to be." and it was an instant attraction.

1 Peter 5:6-7. Humble yourselves, therefore, under God's mighty hand, that he may lift you up in due time. Cast all your anxiety on him because he cares for you.

We started seeing each other every day that summer and then when it was time for me to go back home to Philadelphia we had a long-distance relationship, calling each other every day and seeing each other every weekend for about seven months.

When I got back to Philadelphia after that summer my step father was still there with lust in his eyes. Once he found out I was seeing William my step father started all kinds of trouble, so my mom could hate William. My Mom decided that we couldn't see each other no more and that's when I made my plan to leave. My mother and step father ended up being evicted from the home they were renting, and we ended up split up from each other.

My mother and step father ended up living with my grandfather and my sister Tina ended up living with my aunt Nadine and I ended up living with another uncle my mother's middle brother with my daughter and my three other siblings. I was so angry here I was sixteen years old having to take care of my sisters and brother while my mother and her husband was living it up at my grandfather's home.

You see my mother was always making me responsible for my three other siblings like I was their mother and it made me resentful. I remember times where I would have to stay home from school to watch them because my mother was working, and my step father was nowhere to be seen. I truly resented my mother for that I felt those where her kids and she should have been the one figuring out who would watch them I needed and education. I wanted to go to school.

Well my uncle my mother's middle brother said it was ok for William to come over and see me, so I talked to

William about my plan to leave with my daughter, and he agreed reluctantly only because he was afraid. He called his mom in North Carolina to ask her if he could bring me and my daughter with him down there and his mom said bring them on. I waited until my uncle left to go do his laundry and I made my escape from there. William Got my bags and we got in his car and we left. I ended up going to Atlantic city first to see my grandmother and we told her what we were going to do. She knew what I was going through with my step father, so she agreed for me to go.

She told William he better take care of me and her great granddaughter and if something happens to us she was going to hurt him, and he said yes ma'am I will take good care of them and he did. We stayed in North Carolina for three months and then we moved in with my favorite uncle which was my mother's oldest brother. We lived with him for one year and then we moved out on our own to an efficiency apartment.

Jeremiah 29:11-13 For I know the plans I have for you," declares the Lord, "plans to prosper you and not to harm you, plans to give you hope and a future. Then you will call on me and come and pray to me, and I will listen to you. You will seek me and find me when you seek me with all your heart.

We dated for a total of three years and then we moved to San Diego, California in October of nineteen eighty-seven where we lived together for one year before we decided to get married. What we didn't understand at the time was we were living in sin. As much as we both went to church, William being Baptist and me being Baptist-Catholic, we never heard anything about living in sin or being in sexual sin it seemed back then sex was not talked about in church.

Hebrews 10:26 - For if we sin willfully after that we have received the knowledge of the truth, there remained no more sacrifice for sins,

We were married on February Twenty Eighth Nineteen Eighty-eight and it was such a blessed day. I was so happy, it was just my daughter and I and my new husband present at the wedding. My husband was so nervous that he kept wanting to say I do before the Pastor was finished speaking it was so funny, but we were so proud to be married.

My mother ended up locating us living in San Diego. she moved out there because of some family members we were traveling with. You see when we left Atlantic City to move to San Diego my sister Tina decided she wanted to go with us, so she left home at twelve years old and decided to live with us and I became her guardian, so I put her in school. My Mother came looking for her and all hell broke loose because she was mad that my sister also left home. She came to my home and started a fight between William and uncle Chuck the one I told you about earlier who also molested me and that was it for me. She took Tina to live with her in Los Angeles and for a few days we had not heard from her then.

Tina called us one day while my mother and step father was gone, so William and uncle Nate who molested me in the beginning drove to Los Angeles to go and get her and after that my mother and her husband left us alone. As I told you before God has always spoken to me, I can remember talking to him as young as five years old, so I always knew his voice. One day the Lord spoke to me clear through a dream and said that the reason we were going through all this craziness was because we were living in sin.

I told William, what the Lord said, and we looked it up in the bible and a few weeks later he proposed marriage. That was when we got married. Which I told you about earlier. One year after getting married on the day after our first wedding anniversary we welcomed our first baby boy on March first, nineteen eighty-nine named William Jamal Wright. As time would go on, four years after our first son was born we had a second son born on May twenty Fifth nineteen ninety-three named DeAndre Demetrius Pittman.

We lived in San Diego for nine years before the Lord called us to Orlando, Florida in June 1996. My husband grew up in the church all his life but strayed from the faith as he got older. I went to church and always knew something was watching over me, but I grew up in the North part of Philadelphia which was rough, and I also strayed as I got older. The bible is undoubtedly correct in

Proverbs 22:6 when it says train up a child in the way they should go and when they are old they shall surely not depart from it.

Even after we were married we still didn't always put God first. We were going to the clubs, partying, drinking, and smoking pot. We both suffered from sexual abuse in our childhood and that began affecting us at this point in our marriage. I was so abrasive I would cut you up with my words. I would curse my husband out, and I would curse at the children too if they were doing wrong. My husband would curse like a sailor as well, and we both just didn't have any discretion when it came to our mouth's.

I didn't understand how to be a wife. I mean I seen my mother taking care of us, but when it came to her and her husband they just didn't communicate well. Now on the other hand William saw the loving side of marriage with his grandmother and grandfather. They were married for fifty years, and they demonstrated love towards each other and that's what he desired for us.

Proverbs 18:22. He who finds a wife finds what is good and receives favor from the LORD.

I didn't know how God was going to change our lives, but I'm so glad he did. God soon decided it was time for us to come in from serving the world, even though we were doing all that partying we would still pray together before we went to bed. My husband would initiate prayer, and that was the first time I had ever had a man in my life that wanted to pray, and it was so attractive.

As time went on in our marriage, I still had a soul tie to my daughter's father. I was still in love with him even thou I was already married to my husband. My daughter's father was my first sexual experience, so he was what I called my first love, which I now really see was sin because we were not married. The reason God tells us in the bible in

1 Corinthians 7:2-3 "But since there is so much immorality, each man should have his own wife, and each woman her own husband. The husband should fulfill his marital duty to his wife, and likewise the wife to her husband,"

is because there is no such thing as sex before marriage in his eyes. In the mind of God, sex was created for marriage, not for us to indulge our sinful fantasies.

I believe a lot of our arguments was because I was still in lust for my ex, I say lust because that's what it was. My husband also was still in lust with his ex as well and whenever he got the chance to visit his hometown in North Carolina I knew he would go visit her. I didn't care because I would also go to Philadelphia where I grew up to visit my ex whenever I could.

By the fifth year of our marriage, we both were coming to a real rough patch in our marriage. My husband was working all the time, and I was a stay at home mom until the kids were old enough to go to school. I believe we both were getting bored with the marriage and that's what almost lead us to having affairs.

He was in San Diego when his almost occurred, and I was in Philadelphia visiting when mine almost occurred, but God stopped us both without us knowing the other was about to do the wrong thing. We were constantly arguing and disrespecting each other, it just wasn't working. I still had feelings for my ex, and I felt in my heart my husband still had feelings for his ex. God didn't allow either one of us to commit adultery even though with our hearts we did. You see an emotional affair is still an affair even though there was no sex involved it led to all kinds of disrespect that will lead to arguing.

The bible says in Mathew 5:28 But I tell you that anyone who looks at a woman lustfully has already committed adultery with her in his heart.

We struggled and struggled in our marriage until we both re-dedicated our lives to God back in 1995 which was the seventh year of our marriage. We started attending a church in San Diego called Mesa View Baptist Church where we got baptized and began to give our hearts to God. Even though, we rededicated our lives to Christ we still weren't delivered spiritually, and sometimes we still would drink and go out and smoke pot.

Romans 12:2 - And be not conformed to this world: but be ye transformed by the renewing of your mind, that ye may prove what [is] that good, and acceptable, and perfect, will of God.

We didn't have the knowledge yet for deliverance, so we continued to live like we were. Deliverance from the things you use to do don't come just because you attend church it takes time for anyone to change. if you are going to church and are not yet delivered then keep going until your mind become renewed.

While we were going through our struggles in our marriage, we both began discussing our experiences we had with sexual abuse as I stated earlier we both had been abused as children.

That situation caused me to be angry disrespectful and to hate my body. I believe that the abuse was also a part of our struggles. He was abused by a family friend and then me being abused by my uncles and step- father. It made my husband passive and it made me very angry and aggressive, especially at men and it cause me to be disrespectful towards my husband.

Genesis 50:20 says: You intended to harm me, but God intended it for good to accomplish what is now being done, the saving of many lives.

Getting over sexual abuse is hard especially if you are trying to do it in your own strength that's why we need God and our comforter the Holy Spirit to help us. You see the spirit of fear steps in when these things happen, and when you try to tell someone, and you're not believed, then the spirit of rejection steps in too and so that combination will always cause problems until you conquer it. Not until God called us to Orlando, FL were we able to get free and tell others about what happened.

John 8:36 says: If the Son therefore shall make you free, ye shall be free indeed.

One day about a year before the move God spoke to me in a dream and said I need you to go to Orlando, Florida I have something for you there, so I spoke to my husband, and I told him what God spoke to me and he was just purely against it. I felt in my spirit that even if my husband and I weren't to remain married that I had to do what God said. As I told you earlier, I always knew God's voice, so I packed up my stuff and my kids and moved to Orlando where I stayed with my mother.

Once there I moved my mother from West Orlando to East Orlando where God would build our life, family and ministry. When I got to Orlando, I had a job because I was a hair stylist with JC Penny, and I was able to transfer my job. I only worked there one day when I came across an ad for a stylist job out in Lake Mary. I applied for the job and got it, working for a nursing home called Village on The Green. My husband had stayed in California for three months before he decided he needed to be with his family. God blessed him with a job with UPS that first year of being in Orlando, and suddenly I found out I was pregnant again. We ended up having our daughter a seven-pound six-ounce baby named Takiyah Lashun Denise Pittman on June fifteenth nineteen ninety-nine and we moved into a new home all in a year and a half. We felt this was where God wanted us.

Hebrews 11:8 "By faith Abraham obeyed when he was called to go out to a place that he was to receive as an inheritance. And he went out, not knowing where he was going."

Money was tight even after moving into our new home and we believe it was due to the fact of us not attending services and paying our tithes. Financial management wasn't our strong area we struggled a lot in that area. Orlando was a new city, and we didn't know where to attend church or where to begin paying our tithes, so it took some time to find a church we trusted.

Within that first year of living in Orlando, the devil also tried to kill us in a bad car accident that we had on Econolohochie Trail and Colonial Ave in Orlando, Florida where our car was totaled but God saved us. That accident made us realize that we needed to get back to church serving God and giving back.

"Be self-controlled and alert. Your enemy the devil prowls around like a roaring lion looking for someone to devour. Resist him, standing firm in the faith." 1 Pet. 5:8-9

God guided us to a well-known ministry in the city of Orlando called New Destiny Christian Center where we began our journey of deliverance. God had us under some awesome pastors, Pastor Reva and Zachary Tim's. It was there God began to deliver us from selfishness, unkindness, unloving and mean attitudes towards each other and our past of sexual abuse.

As the young pastors taught on different things and as we served, God began to show us that in our current spiritual condition we could not inherit what he had for us, so we desperately needed a change as husband and wife and as a family.

God began to filter out of me what I was taught as a young lady as to how to treat a man. There was never an example in front of me as to be a "submissive" wife and so because of that I just hated that word. In my family, we were taught to be the boss of the man and that things will go my way and not his. I was also taught not to be a punk to a man, my mother would always say and somehow, I just knew that was wrong. I did as I was taught thinking it was right so as the young pastors began to teach, I began to see that the way I was taught was less than God's best for me.

Now my husband always seen his grandfather work hard, and his grandmother be at home cooking and raising the kids, which I did when we were living in California for nine years. Even though my husband was good at working, and I was good at cooking and raising the kids, it still was a struggle because our communication skills towards each other at times were horrible.

While we were attending this worldwide church, God set me up for my deliverance little did I know that there was going to be a women's conference in Tampa fl. A prophetess who I was following on TV was going to be in Tampa, and I had known of her ministry through TBN the Trinity Broadcasting Network and her name was Juanita Bynum. She was having a conference called Women Weapons of Power conference back in 2002. I told God I would really like to go to this conference, but I didn't have any money or a way there. God used some of my beautiful sisters in Christ at New Destiny Christian

Center, who were going and had an extra ticket invite me to go all-expenses-paid.

Proverbs 18:16 says ESV: A man's gift makes room for him and brings him before the great.

God made a way for my deliverance, and he delivered me, at that conference. I married God at that conference back in August 2002. After the conference, God said, "Loretta you are the biggest influence in your home and when you get back home if you let me change you I will change your whole house" meaning my immediate family," and that's when our real marriage journey began.

Isaiah 54:5 ESV. For your Maker is your husband, the Lord of hosts is his name; and the Holy One of Israel is your Redeemer, the God of the whole earth he is called.

God gave me a book called **The Power of a Praying Wife** through one of my sisters in Christ, and he began to have me pray for the things I wanted changed in my husband. The things I began to pray for God began to do those changes in me. As I began on a journey of change with God, I began to be real sensitive to not only the spirit but also to the negative words of my husband. It seemed that he was being mean and nasty to me when really that was how we were communicating all along. His words were cutting me like a knife, but God was allowing him to be that way because that was the way we both were I didn't see it until the holy spirit entered in because I was spiritually blind. You see when your spiritually blind you say and do all kinds of disrespectful things and that's how the devil wants you to be blind.

As God took us on this journey and this process I felt like things were never going to change. The more I prayed for him the worst things seemed to get. Little did I know that it would be eleven more years of this process before change would come. Believe me it was the roughest time of my life. I was truly in the fire, and my husband was the coal miner. He would say something nasty to me, and I would say something nasty back. The more I said something nasty God would say, "No, go back in your prayer closet you're not ready yet," and I would say, "But God didn't you hear what he said to me?" and God would say, "No, it's you. You're not submissive, so go back and pray." I would be in prayer sometimes for hours. Just crying and praying and crying and praying this went on from Two Thousand Two to Two thousand three.

One day I discovered Freda Bowers on channel WACX-TV in Orlando, she wrote a book called Give Me 40 Days and I began fasting and praying. I made a deal with God that I would fast by getting up at 5am every morning to talk to him, pray and read this book Give Me 40 Days, and that's what broke this negative and disrespectful spirit I had towards my husband.

The word says in Mark 29:9 And he said unto them, this kind can come forth by nothing, but by prayer and fasting.

I gave God 40 days more to deliver me, and he did! God showed me himself on the last day of my fast.

We had just come back from a conference called He Did It in The Name of Love at Johnathan McKnight church when I had this open and very real experience with God. God came to me in a form of a heavy white cloud and at first, I was scared until God said, "Don't be afraid it's just me," then after the cloud I saw a flash of constant light that was very warm like sun rays and it went up and down my body. I could feel him healing my mind, body, and soul it was fascinating, and this went on it seemed for a long time, but it was short and then the light just went away. Right after that I truly knew God was real, and I was healed and delivered.

One thing I didn't mention was that the time between 2002 and 2003 God was taking us through the process of deliverance. He was delivering us from all those other spirits we were dealing with such as witchcraft. I was dealing in tarot cards and seeing physics not knowing it was of the devil (I was still operating from that lack of knowledge point). That was also a family thing growing up my grandmother seen physics and my aunts. My mother took me to see my first physic when I was sixteen. I guess that was all they knew about getting answers to life's problems. They didn't understand that you can't mix witchcraft with God darkness and light can't mix.

John 18:12 ESV says: Again, Jesus spoke to them, saying, "I am the light of the world. Whoever follows

me will not walk in darkness but will have the light of life."

I fell deep into it to the point of telling my friends and co- workers their fortunes and I was very good at it not knowing that my real gift was prophesy. The devil was trying to use my gift for his glory, but I know now that the devil is a liar! It took a good friend of mine name Patricia Allen from San Diego, CA to tell me I was doing wrong and once she read me the scriptures about witchcraft I threw everything away, and I renounced the spirit of witchcraft and then the devil came after us.

My husband and I went through night after night of some intense spiritual warfare. The devil was mad that we were heading for deliverance, and he didn't want that. It seemed like we were fighting those demons for a long time but after that we were delivered and saved and set free and speaking in tongues and seeing, hearing and healing in the spirit we now belonged to God and the devil could no longer stop us. Believe me God will always equip you with more knowledge when God allows you to come through a situation. Now we were well on our way to the victory. Even though God was taking us through this process, our season was up, and he released us from New Destiny Christian Center.

Luke 9:1 And He called the twelve together and gave them power and authority over all the demons and to heal diseases.

We began attending a church called World Wide Deliverance Ministries for one year where we would be ordained and sent out to build the ministry God gave us called New Covenant of Faith Int'l Ministries. In October two thousand and four, we began to hold services in a building on Fairmont Ave in Winter Park that we called the upper room that's because it was literally one room. I had a salon God blessed me with also at that time that was right underneath the upper room. In the process God gave us a food pantry ministry where we would partner with the supermarkets and stores in Orlando. We would go out and give the food away to the different organizations as well as to the homeless in the woods.

God gave us a furniture ministry where we would furnish the homes of those in need. The furniture ministry was a result of God telling us to give away all our furniture we just bought. In our process, God was teaching us how to give away big things not just money, but what we held dear to us. Ever since God told us to give away that furniture we have never had a want for furniture no more. Now God was moving, and it was awesome.

Luke 10:1-3 Now after this the Lord appointed seventy others and sent them in pairs ahead of Him to every city and place where He Himself was going to come.

God gave us the vision and told us to build. He led us to fill the space we were holding service in more than once. Then God opened the door for us to minister to the youth in jail over in Sanford, FL. That was when true healing of our sexual abuse was a reality because we were now ministering to the youth and telling them about how we were sexually abused which lead to my promiscuity and then being pregnant at 15. It was truly liberating, and it was the first time I shared that with anyone in our church. There wasn't a dry eye in that place it really blessed the youth to hear that because some of them were going through that. We as parents need to find out why our children are acting out, we should not assume that they are just bad but find out what the real problem is, could it be they are being abused by someone you trust, and you don't know it?

Ecclesiastes 4:1 ESV. Again, I saw all the oppressions that are done under the sun. And behold, the tears of the oppressed, and they had no one to comfort them! On the side of their oppressors there was power, and there was no one to comfort them.

God also allowed us to minister on WOKB radio in Orlando for three years and one year on Rejoice 1140 am. One year before God was to have us to leave Orlando he began to deal with my husband.

Acts 1:8 but you will receive power when the Holy Spirit has come upon you; and you shall be My witnesses both in Jerusalem, and in all Judea and Samaria, and even to the remotest part of the earth."

The Lord gave me a book called **The Power of a Praying Wife** when he was processing me as I told you earlier and I used those prayers to pray for my husband. As things progressed my husband saw the changes in me and he wanted to be changed too, so God led him to get the book **The Power of a Praying Husband** and as he prayed for me God began to change those things in him, and then we both began to get dreams from God of becoming one. The more we prayed for each other, the more we changed and the more we became one.

1Peter 3:1-6 In the same way, you wives, be submissive to your own husbands so that even if any of them are disobedient to the word, they may be won without a word by the behavior of their wives, as they observe your chaste and respectful behavior.

In February two thousand and ten God sent us here to Upper Darby Pennsylvania, which was something my husband did not want he always hated Philly, and he vowed never to return here. One night we went to a service at One Accord Ministries (Pastor Roberto) in Orlando and received a prophecy we weren't looking for. The prophesy was we were going to move up north and five years to the day of receiving that prophecy God showed us in a dream that it was time to go.

Luke 10:1-3 Now after this the Lord appointed seventy others, and sent them in pairs ahead of Him to every city and place where He Himself was going to come

When God told us to leave to go to Philadelphia, they just had the worst snow storm ever. We looked at each other and said God are you serious, but we packed and off we went. When we moved here, it was one of the scariest actions of faith we ever experienced.

The first couple of months was fine God showed us favor with man. We asked God what he wanted us to do here and we just kept going back to the dreams and the prophecy that God showed us as we kept the faith. It was rough, but I also felt it was testing time. We lived out of hotel rooms until there was no more money. Although my husband was finding odd jobs it still wasn't enough to cover living expenses and food so for three months, we lived in our truck as we prayed and blamed one another for this homeless situation. We found a church, and we attended whenever they had service.

I had an aunt that lived here but she couldn't take us in because she was a live-in worker herself, but she was a great help financially. It still wasn't enough to have a place. All I can say is even though we were now living in our truck God never let us go hungry, and we were able to go to a clean McDonalds where we washed up and changed our clothes. At night we would park at the McDonalds to sleep. My husband and I would keep watch over our family so we all could get some rest, but little did we know this situation would totally deliver our marriage and bring us closer together as a family. My son was being plagued by demons and he was delivered; our constant arguing was now delivered, and our borrowing was also delivered?

Galatians 5:1 It is for freedom that Christ has set us free. Stand firm, then, and do not let yourselves be burdened again by a yoke of slavery.

God spoke to us to not to borrow one more dime from no one and that he would take care of us and he did. God had us go on food stamps and then one of our friends who we used to attend church with in Orlando was in contact with us while we were going through this situation. Unbeknownst to us she called one of her friends who lived in Philly and asked her and her husband to help us even though she didn't know what we were going through. The lady called me, and I called her back. She invited us over and we told her and her husband our testimony. The lady and her husband proceeded to pray for God's will to be done. They offered for us to stay with them temporarily, so we could get things together and we stayed there almost three months.

One of the brothers in Christ at the church we were attending called Living Faith Christian Center in Pennsauken NJ had a rooming house that was just for men. But he made an exception for us because we were a family.

It was a big room with air conditioning that is rare in the city of Philadelphia, but we could now see the hand of God and that things were getting better. My husband met this pastor who sent him to this apartment complex for what he thought was a lawn service contract, but God had a job for him instead. He applied, and they hired him, but little did we know that the property they sent him to work at was one of the property's we visited while we were homeless.

Philippians 4:1 And my God will supply all your needs according to His riches in glory in Christ Jesus.

We were thinking we were just going to be blessed with a place to live there, but it was way too expensive, so we left and now we were back because that was where my husband was going to work. After my husband got the job God began to show us in a dream that he was going move us into a house, and he did. We lived in that room three months, and we saved to move into this house. We lived there one year and then God moved us from Philadelphia to where he told us we would live, and that was Drexel Hill/Upper Darby Pa. We are now right smack dead in God's will living between Owens Ave and Garret Rd. The land I was spying out before we got here in Pennsylvania from the dream he gave us and the prophecy five years earlier. We were in awe but happy none the less.

Back in two thousand and nine before we got here to Philly the Marriage Café began to be birthed. It was just an idea we had out of our desire to help struggling marriages be delivered and healed. Little did we know that it would be two more years before we were ready to launch our new baby?

On February twenty third two thousand and eleven we opened a Facebook account and placed our first post, and this is what it said, "Hello all this is Prophetess and Bishop Pittman's new baby Marriage Cafe we are a forum that is here to help marriages heal from past hurts." God has healed us and restored our marriage, and we want to use our marriage to help heal and restore other's marriages. We launched Marriage Café on Blog Talk Radio on March fourth two thousand and eleven and then on March seventh two thousand and eleven. We also launched it on Ustream.

On August fourth two thousand and eleven Marriage Wisdom was birthed and now here we are today. I began writing about our struggles and our pain as the Holy Spirit directed me too and God told me to call it Marriage Wisdom, and this is how this book came about. When I learned that Facebook was doing a timeline from when the page started until now that's when I realized, I had a book. I didn't know that all that time I spent writing about my pain that it was all saved. I could now go back and retrieve all that information that was previously written so that I could place it in a book that we now call **A Cup of Daily Wisdom for Your Marriage.**

We are now so happy and so in love and so grateful to God for this process it is a continual process, but I thank God for where we are in our marriage today.

Without going through that process, we wouldn't be where we are today, and I can honestly say that we are in an awesome place in our marriage. I can now truly say I love the word submissive. God has truly taught me the meaning of being submissive. I am now in my proper place as a wife and mother and my husband is in his place as the Priest and Father and our grown children know their place.

God is so good, and he can change anybody if he can change our marriage and change us he can change anyone and any situation. All we must do is be willing to submit to the process of what God wants. God taught me that if I could be submissive to him whom I can't see why is it that I can't be submissive to my husband whom I can see.

We must know that as husbands and wives we are to trust the God in our spouses, but we are to rely on God to be everything to us. We need to learn to become one with the Holy Spirit, who is our comforter and is always with us he'll never leave us nor forsake us.

My husband and I have been married now for thirty years and he is my best friend, and I am so in love with him. Our marriage is better than it's ever been.

We're here to help as many marriages stay together and keep the covenant that God has given them and learn how to stay in the fire with each other no matter what! It's about endurance, and that's what God has taught us we will follow him until glory comes.

We pray our story is a source of inspiration for those reading this book. Our Prayer is that this book will save and deliver as many marriages as it possibly can for the Glory of God! **Be Blessed!**

WISDOM ON LOVE
CHAPTER 1

Marriage Wisdom Moment: Day 1

Ephesians 5:25. Husbands love your wives even as Christ also loved the church and gave himself for it.

In other words, husbands don't say you love your wife when you talk to her in a nasty tone. A true and loving husband will lead by example so whatever you want your wife to do for you do it for her first and reap the rewards. **Be Blessed!**

Marriage Wisdom Moment: Day 2

Ephesians 4:32. And be kind to one another tenderhearted forgiving one another even as God for Christ sake has forgiven you.

In other words, husbands and wives when you have a disagreement be the first to forgive. It doesn't make you weak to ask for forgiveness that's just that prideful spirit that wants to keep negativity going. If you love each other, you can forgive each other's shortcomings. **Be Blessed!**

Marriage Wisdom Moment: Day 3

Genesis 2:22. And the rib which the Lord God had taken from man he made into a woman and brought her to the man.

In other words, your wife is the missing rib God took from Adam, so if that is true why would husbands not want to take care of their wives? Do you take care of your body? You don't hit yourself or beat yourself or talk to yourself like trash. The next time you think about doing these things to your wife think of her as being your missing rib. **Be Blessed!**

Marriage Wisdom Moment: Day 4

Amos 3:3. Can two walk together unless they have agreed to do so?

In other words, what can the married couple do to ensure that their marriage will last? The first and most important issue is one of obedience to God and his word. This is a principle that should be enforce before marriage. For the born-again believer this means not being too close with anyone who is not also a believer as well as being on one accord with each other. **Be Blessed!**

Marriage Wisdom Moment: Day 5

Mathew 19:6. So they are no longer two but one therefore what God has joined together let no man separate.

In other words, never let anyone speak negative or come between your marriage and you. God should be the only one speaking into your marriage. Stop discussing your problems with people who cannot help you especially those of a single nature. **Be Blessed!**

Marriage Wisdom Moment: Day 6

Proverbs 18:22. He who finds a wife, find a good thing and obtained the favor from the Lord.

In other words, if God has blessed you with finding a wife she is your good thing and God gives you favor because of her. Remember man of God that your wife is a gift from God to you so don't just treat her any kind of way and speak to her any kind of way. Remember God designed her just for you and he knows her better than you, so ask God today how to please her, and he will show you how. Remember you wouldn't have favor without her. **Be Blessed!**

Marriage Wisdom Moment: Day 7

Proverbs 8:17. I love those who love me, and those who seek me early and diligently shall find me.

In other words, if you are a married couple seeking God for your marriage then you must love him and therefore you shall find him. He says seek him early because that's when he will be found. If you have been seeking God for an answer to your prayers then love him, seek him early and be diligent and your prayer shall be answered. Don't make God your last resort put him first! **Be Blessed!**

Marriage Wisdom Moment: Day 8

Proverbs 18:21. Death and life be in the power of the tongue, and those who love it will eat its fruits.

In other words, today is a blessed day to speak blessings over your spouse and over your family. The word says life and death are in the power of the tongue. Today is the day to declare that the rest of your year will be the best of your year. No matter what is going on remember adversity is only a stepping stone to the blessing so don't get mad get glad! **Be Blessed!**

Marriage Wisdom Moment: Day 9

Proverbs 1:28 and 29. Then they will call to me, but I will not answer; they will look for me but will not find me since they hated knowledge and did not fear the Lord.

In other words, get your marriage knowledge from the word and not from the world. God is the one who designed marriage so why search the world for something only God knows. Let the word of God be your marriage guide. If you don't seek God for your answers, you will not find them. Listen to the word of God, and he will answer any problems you have. **Be Blessed!**

Marriage Wisdom Moment: Day 10

Proverbs 10:27. The reverent and worshipful fear of the Lord prolongs one's days, but the years of the wicked shall be made short.

In other words, when we live and love in the Lord, which is worshipful fear we will live a long and happy life. Those who live and love in wickedness their days will be cut short on this earth. We should be living and loving in the Lord so, we will have long and blessed marriages, but if our marriage is of the world then don't expect it to last long. God owns all things including the devil, so don't you owe it to yourself to give your marriage a chance for longevity by making God the head of your marriage think about it. **Be Blessed!**

Marriage Wisdom Moment: Day 11

Mathew 7:24. Everyone then who hears these words of mine and does them will be like a wise man who built his house on the rock.

In Other words, Take the time today to build your marriage on the rock the Lord Jesus Christ. While you are building that relationship build your personal relationship with the father. You must know how to get into his presence and listen for his voice and obey what he asked of you. Start by making God your, everything that means you will do nothing without talking to him about it first. Give him the first part of your day instead of the last and give him the first seed before paying everyone else and watch how he will make you and your situation and your finances first on his kingdom list.
Be Blessed!

Marriage Wisdom Moment: Day 12

Colossians 13:18-19. Wives, submit to your husbands, as is fitting for those who belong to the Lord. Husbands love your wives and never treat them harshly

In other words, Marriage is a gift from God, and we ought to treat it as such. God is so good that to keep his children from being in sin and to teach his children how to love he made marriage. Don't ever look at your marriage as just an agreement on a piece of paper think of your spouse and family as a gift because that's what it is. **Be Blessed!**

Marriage Wisdom Moment: Day 13

Matthew 19:6. Wherefore they are no more twain, but one flesh. What therefore, God hath joined together, let not man put asunder.

In other words, Marriage is not just something you do it's a covenant relationship that you enter in the sight of God. Don't you owe it to yourself to find out what it really means to be married? The covenant contract tells you everything in the bible look it up. **Be Blessed!**

Marriage Wisdom Moment: Day 14

Ephesians 5:21. Submitting yourselves one to another in the fear of God.

In other words, sometimes in marriage we must submit to what our spouses want to do. It's not always about us and it may be something you really don't want to do. How can you submit to God whom you cannot see and can't submit to the spouse you can see? Try it any way and you may find that it wasn't so bad after all. **Be Blessed!**

Marriage Wisdom Moment: Day 15

Isaiah 51:11. Those the LORD has rescued will return. They will enter Zion with singing; everlasting joy will crown their heads. Gladness and joy will overtake them, and sorrow and sighing will flee away.

In other words, we as married couples need to learn how to have fun. Marriage shouldn't always be so serious we need to learn to enjoy what God has given us. If we speak blessings over our marriages, we will have blessings so have fun and enjoy each other! **Be Blessed!**

Marriage Wisdom Moment: Day 16

Romans 15:7. Accept one another, then, just as Christ accepted you, to bring praise to God.

In other words, the key to a long-lasting marriage is to stop trying to change the other person, just love that person for who they are and accept them the way they are. Pray for God to make you both one and accept the challenges that come your way. Remember whatever he or she is lacking you make it up as their spouse that's what make you one in the first place. **Be Blessed!**

Marriage Wisdom Moment: Day 17

Romans 5:3. We can rejoice, too, when we run into problems and trials for we know that they help us develop endurance.

In other words, every marriage goes through growing pains, but in your pain, is where you learn the best lessons. Don't look at your pain as the end of your marriage look at it as the beginning of learning something else new you didn't know about your spouse. Marriage is an awesome institution for learning. **Be Blessed!**

Marriage Wisdom Moment: Day 18

1st Corinthians 13:4 –8 NIV. Love suffers long and is kind; love does not envy, love does not promote itself, is not puffed up, does not behave badly, seeks not her own, is not easily provoked, thinks no evil, does not rejoice in iniquity, but rejoices in the truth, bears all things, believes all things, hope all things, endure all things love never fails. Marriage should look like this.

In other words, love is not selfish and does not envy and is not jealous. If you married the right person you don't need to be controlling and jealous over your spouse. Love does not hurt us love should feel good. Our spouses should love us the way God does. **Be Blessed!**

Date night
Let's Get Started!

Date night is of the utmost importance to have a marriage of longevity. The reason we suggest date night is because if there is no marriage there is no family. Choose what you might want to do for your date night the tips we have suggested are just that! Suggestions! We just want to get the sparks flying on what to do. Planning will always be the #1 key to a successful marriage; you planned your wedding now let's plan to succeed in your marriage. Putting God first in your marriage is also a must to succeed and to pray for each other every day is also a must. Be creative and don't do the same things twice unless you both enjoy it. These are the rules for date night

Date Night Simplified!

1. Put God first
2. Date Night is a must
3. Praying for each other every day is a must
4. Planning is always #1 you must plan to have a successful night
5. be creative don't be repetitive unless you both enjoy it.

Lee & Felissa's Story

Lee and I met through his younger brother. Lee was just coming home from Theology College in Oklahoma when one day I was at the corner store and Lee and his brother saw me. I never saw Lee, he asked his brother who was I, and he said oh she is my classmate and a young lady I am saving for myself. Lee asked if he knew where I lived, and can he please take him to my house. His brother hesitated and said ok, so within an hour after I came home from the store I get a knock at the door. It was Lee's younger brother and he said my brother would like to meet you and then he asked if he could come over to see me from time to time. We went on a few dates and within a month he bought me a promise ring and asked if I would marry him when I turned eighteen I was sixteen at the time, and I said yes.

A prophet came to visit our church in New York, and he said God told him to tell us that our marriage was arranged when we were in our mother's womb. Our marriage hasn't always been easy, but I thank God for everything. At this point in life, I feel like our marriage is stronger because we are older and wiser now. We are still in love with each other after all these years. Our sex life is even better because of wisdom and maturity. We were married July second nineteen eighty-eight, and we have been married for Twenty-Five years now. This year Twenty fourteen will make Twenty-six years. We just thank God for keeping our marriage. God is the head of our marriage, and it's him who helps your marriage last. Trust God and his infinite wisdom

WISDOM ON COMMUNICATION
CHAPTER 2

Marriage Wisdom Moment: Day 19

Galatians: 6:7-8. "Be not deceived; God is not mocked: for whatsoever a man soweth, that shall he also reap. For he that soweth to his flesh shall of the flesh reap corruption; but he that soweth to the Spirit shall of the Spirit reap life everlasting."

In other words, if you want your spouse to treat you a certain way then start treating him or her that way in advance, and you will get what you want. Remember what God said whatever a man sows that he shall also reap! So, if you're sowing anger you will reap anger it's bound to come back. Sow what you desire. **Be Blessed!**

Marriage Wisdom Moment: Day 20

Malachi 2:14. The Lord has been witnessed between you and the wife of your youth, against whom you have dealt treacherously: yet she's your companion and the wife of your covenant.

In other words, stop being selfish in your marriage if you are using sex, money or the divorce word to get your way you are selfish. You are in a holy covenant with God as the head of that covenant, so you need to take the marriage and the way you treat each other more seriously. **Be Blessed!**

Marriage Wisdom Moment: Day 21

Proverbs 14:1. Every wise woman built her house, but the foolish one tears it down with her own hands.

In other words, we as women and wives are the biggest influences in our homes with our husbands, kids and in our marriages. We should not be bringing strife, jealousy and negativity in our homes and then use it against our family, therefore, tearing down our home. Just because your friends are having problems in their home doesn't mean you should bring their problems to your home. Be wise don't bring someone else's stuff into your home keep the peace. **Be Blessed!**

Marriage Wisdom Moment: Day 22

Genesis 2:7. And the LORD God formed man [of] the dust of the ground, and breathed into his nostrils the breath of life, and man became a living soul.

In other words, God created us in his image and therefore our first relationship should be to him. If a man or woman don't have a relationship with God how do you expect for them to have one with you! Our marriage should reflect our relationship with our heavenly father hello! **Be Blessed!**

Marriage Wisdom Moment: Day 23

Malachi 2:13. Has not the one God made you? You belong to him in body and spirit. And what does the one God seek? Godly offspring. So be on your guard and do not be unfaithful to the wife of your youth.

In other words, the condition of your marriage is also the condition of the relationship you have with God. If your marriage is not good, it's because your relationship with God is not good. God need married couples to be faithful and Godly, so we can have Godly children. We need to have a relationship with God to remain faithful and Godly. Get with God today and repent and start a love affair with him your marriage and family depends on it! **Be Blessed!**

Marriage Wisdom Moment: Day 24

Proverbs 27:15. A continual dropping on a very rainy day and an argumentative woman are alike.

In other words, women play a very important part in the home and in the marriage, and if you are always argumentative then, you are bringing strife into your home. Figure out why you are so argumentive have other relationships hurt you? Is it a learned behavior from your mom or other women of influence in your life? Find out what the real problem is and take it to God in prayer. Start praying about what you are arguing about and let God work it out. Let God help you be successful in the most important part you play in your life and family every day. **Be Blessed!**

Marriage Wisdom Moment: Day 25

Proverbs 25:28. He that hath no rule over his spirit is like a city that is broken down without walls.

In other words, you are in control of the way you treat your husband or your wife. God is watching how you control your spirit in different situations that occur in your marriage. Stop blaming your bad attitude on your husband or your wife get control of yourself and decide to keep a good Godly spirit. **Be Blessed!**

Marriage Wisdom Moment: Day 26

Proverbs 10:22. The blessings of the Lord make rich, and he adds no sorrow with it.

In other words, when the Lord blesses you, you will not be sorry he did. If your marriage is from God, then you shouldn't be sorry you married your husband or wife. Yes, every marriage has its ups and downs, but that's just part of the process of becoming one. Stop complaining about your spouse and begin to pray for them. God knows them better than you. You won't be sorry you did. **Be Blessed!**

Marriage Wisdom Moment: Day 27

Proverbs 15:28. The mind of the righteous studies how to answer but the mouth of the wicked pours out evil things.

In other words, husbands and wives need to learn how to answer each other in love. At some point in your marriage, you should know the habits of each other to the point of knowing what he or she will say next. Once you learn your spouse's ways don't keep flying off the handle. If we love God, we will keep strife down by answering with a loving, answer not argumentative. Learn how to answer by studying your partner. **Be Blessed!**

Marriage Wisdom Moment: Day 28

Proverbs 7:4. Say to the skillful and godly wisdom, you are my sister and regard understanding or insight as your intimate friend.

In other words, love godly wisdom and understanding like, you love the people in your life. Wisdom come from the mistakes we make and learn from in our walk with God. As a married couple, we should constantly be learning from and about one another that's how we learn how to please one another in marriage. Don't be afraid of making mistakes just learn from them and when you do make a mistake use it as wisdom to help someone else. **Be Blessed!**

Marriage Wisdom Moment: Day 29

Proverbs 9:9. Give instruction to a wise man, and he will be yet wiser; teach a righteous man and he will increase in learning.

In other words, when we give advice to a wise person they will be even wiser by what was said, and it will increase his learning. Now how come when our spouses are telling us something that they do or don't like we, are not listening to what is being said. If we take the time to listen to one another we will increase our learning about each other. It's funny how we will take the time to study books in school or read books about marriage when all you must do is just listen. Take the time today to hear and study what your spouse is saying and then begin doing what they ask and watch how it will change your relationship. **Be Blessed!**

Marriage Wisdom Moment: Day 30

Proverbs 12:4. A virtuous and worthy wife is a crowning joy to her husband, but she who makes him ashamed is as rottenness in his bones.

In other words, are you that woman who is loud and belligerent and just downright ugly to your husband in public or in front of his friends and family? If so, then the Scripture is talking about you. Men don't like no loud, argumentative woman yelling at him in front of your friends, his friends, and family even just in public with others. A man need respect no matter what! Take the time today to learn how to be a respectful wife and be a virtuous wife. If you don't know how just ask God to transform you and he will. A man need to know he's the man. **Be Blessed!**

Marriage Wisdom Moment: Day 31

Proverbs 13:5. A righteous man hates lying and deceit, but a wicked man is a loathsome (his very breath spreads pollution), and he comes shortly to shame.

In other words, if you are a true man or woman of God you don't have to lie about anything, but a person whose wicked they are liars and the people they keep company with are liars. If you are a couple who keeps company with people who are liars and deceivers and those who start trouble then, you're just like they are birds of a feather flock together. Check the folks you call your friends, if they are liars and deceivers help them get delivered today by confronting them and then pray for them that they will seek the truth in every situation. Don't be a husband and wife who lie to one another, remember when we lie to one another were lying to God because he gave you your spouse. **Be Blessed!**

Marriage Wisdom Moment: Day 32

Proverbs 8:35. For whoever finds wisdom finds life and draws forth and obtained favor from the Lord.

In other words, seek God's wisdom in all situations especially in marriage. Sometimes you think it's okay just to go with the flow and do what you feel is right, but God says seek first the kingdom. When making decisions in marriage seek God's wisdom first, wait on the answer and then proceed, you wouldn't make a business transaction without thinking about it first would you? **Be Blessed!**

Marriage Wisdom Moment: Day 33

Proverbs 21:30 there is no human wisdom or understanding or counsel that can prevail against the Lord.

In other words, God is the only one who can solve your problems. Don't seek worldly wisdom for your marriage the world can't comprehend the institution of a Godly marriage only our heavenly father can. **Be Blessed!**

Marriage Wisdom Moment: Day 34

Proverbs 22:1. A good name is to be chosen rather than great riches loving favor rather than silver and gold.

In other words, choose to have a good name rather than just wanting to have a lot of money. Your character as a married couple is so important to God. What are people saying about you? Are you being a good example for others or do people cringe when they see you? Keep the integrity in your marriage and model your marriage by the word of God. The Bible tells you how to be in a marriage. If you're going to make a name for yourself let it be honorable. **Be Blessed!**

Marriage Wisdom Moment: Day 35

Proverbs: 2:20. So you walk in the way of good men and keep to the path of the righteous.

In other words, who you keep company with as a married couple is so important to God. You should keep company with those that are of God and are positive as well as married. We as married couples should not have separate friends from our spouses, and we shouldn't always keep company with our single friends knowing that they like to hang out in places we as married couples shouldn't be. Ask God for married godly friends that can help you as a married couple go to another level in him. If your friends come to you for advice all the time, then it's time for some new friends that can pour into you and your marriage. **Be Blessed!**

Marriage Wisdom Moment: Day 36

Proverbs 19:14. House of riches are the inheritance from fathers, but a wise understanding and the prudent wife is from the Lord.

In other words, be that wife that is spiritually smart knowing that everything you have come from God your family, finances, home and life. Giving God all praises and honor because when you honor God you will honor your husband and love your family. Take the time today to bless and honor your husband. Tell him something you've never told him before or cook him a nice meal. Do something you've never done before he will love and honor you for it. **Be Blessed!**

Marriage Wisdom Moment: Day 37

Proverbs 30:24 – 28. There are four things that are little in the earth, but they are exceedingly wise. The ants are a people both strong, yet they lay up their food in the summer (prepared), the conies are but a feeble folk, yet they make their houses in the rocks (stand on the word). The locusts have no king, yet they go forth all of them by bands (work together), and the lizard you can seize with your hands, yet it is in the king's palaces (fearless thinking).

In other words, these are the components of what we need as a married couple to succeed in marriage #1. Prepare together, #2. Stand on the word, # 3. Work together and #4. No fear. **Be Blessed!**

Marriage Wisdom Moment: Day 38

Proverbs 19:2. Desire without knowledge is not good, and to be overhasty is to sin and missed the mark.

In other words, to want something without knowing about it and have an understanding about it but don't pray about it then go and get it is a sin to God and it won't be successful. Now you women who want to be married need to stop wanting and start learning how to be a wife and what it takes to stand when your husband don't act right.

For you women who just ran out and got any man and married him without learning about him and want God's blessings it will not be successful. Especially if that man does not know God and is not submitted unto him. For those of us who are married and have God's blessings keep learning one another. Don't be so hasty to get a divorce pray for them more and know what God put together let no man put asunder! **Be Blessed!**

Marriage Wisdom Moment: Day 39

Proverbs 1:5. A wise man will hear and will increase learning, and a man of understanding shall attain unto wise counsels.

In other words, we should always be learning from our mistakes and a lot of times we make many mistakes until we learn how to come into oneness in marriage. When we do have a problem don't always want to quit the marriage because it seems, we've gotten too far in anger or feel that your marriage can't get past that situation. Seek wise counsel when you need help. Don't quit over every problem just know this too shall pass. **Be Blessed!**

Marriage Wisdom Moment: Day 40

Ephesians 5:25. Husbands love your wife as Christ loved the church husbands are supposed to be communicating with God to get knowledge and understanding on how to please his wife.

In other words, we as husbands and wives should know everything about each other no one should be able to tell you something about one another without your knowledge. Watch those who try to come in and cause division even in the church. Husbands keep your mind; body and spirit on your own wife and wives do the same for your own husband. **Be Blessed!**

Marriage Wisdom Moment: Day 41

Jeremiah 29:11 for I know the plans I have for you," declares the LORD, "plans to prosper you and not to harm you, plans to give you hope and a future.

In other words, is your marriage yielded to God for his glory? Or is your marriage just for your own selfish reasons? Don't you know God has a plan for your marriage? He wants to use your marriage to minister to someone else's marriage, so they can help someone else. You owe it to God to find out how he wants to use your marriage so when you go to pray, Pray God's will be done in your marriage, so it can be used for his glory! We are all here to touch each other's lives in some way. Yield your marriage to him today and let God change it in ways you never thought he could. **Be Blessed!**

Marriage Wisdom Moment: Day 42

Galatians 5:22. But the fruit of the Spirit is love, joy, peace, forbearance, kindness, goodness, faithfulness, gentleness and self-control.

In other words, do you know that marriage teaches us the fruits of the spirit? love, joy, peace, happiness, long-suffering, self-control, and faithfulness goodness and kindness without these we cannot be like God? That's why we should never give up on our spouses they help us to be more like our heavenly father. The process of marriage is not always peachy, but God promises us the victory and the blessing in the end. Don't let little things spoil your marriage stay focused and let God lead. A marriage built on the rock (Jesus Christ) will always be successful no matter what! **Be Blessed!**

Marriage Wisdom Moment: Day 43

Proverbs 10:24. What the wicked dread will overtake them; what the righteous desire will be granted.

In other words, sometimes what we fear can come upon us, so you want to cast down the spirit of fear. If we are children of God, there is no fear because we know that our heavenly father will take care of us. He didn't die for us to be afraid! So instead of being in fear know the promises and wait upon them, remember that the desires of the righteous shall be granted. You haven't missed God! **Be Blessed!**

Marriage Wisdom Moment: Day 44

Proverbs 4:23. Keep your heart with all diligence, for out of it spring the issues of life.

In other words, as married couples we need to watch what we say to each other. We must remember whatever is in our hearts will come out of our mouths so ask God to change what you think about your spouse especially if it's negative and disrespectful. Whatever you are saying about your spouse you are saying about yourself remember you are one. **Be Blessed!**

Marriage Wisdom Moment: Day 45

Proverbs 12:16. From the fruit of their lips, people are filled with good things, and the work of their hands bring them a reward.

In other words, what we declare with our mouths in our marriage is what will come to pass. We are the captains of our ship especially in marriage if we say we will have a beautiful day then you will have one. In a marriage, you must declare the things you want to happen and then work together toward the desired end. Whatever you want in your marriage it will happen, speak blessings over your marriage, and you shall have it. God is so awesome giving us such power! **Be Blessed!**

Marriage Wisdom Moment: Day 46

Proverbs 18:7. "Fool's mouth is his destruction, and his lips are the snare of his soul."

In other words, don't you know your words have power? Be careful next time you're in a disagreement with your spouse because those words have a way of coming to life. If you say something you don't mean especially to or about your spouse stop and rebuke it and ask God for forgiveness, so that thing don't come to pass. **Be Blessed!**

Marriage Wisdom Moment: Day 47

Ephesians 5:33. However, each one of you also must love his wife as he loves himself, and the wife must respect her husband.

In other words, Communication is key to any marriage if you don't communicate you will have a breakdown in your relationship. How's your communication with God? Is it broken, or does it need to be fixed? If so fix it by getting into a relationship with God, so you won't have a breakdown in your marriage. **Be Blessed!**

Marriage Wisdom Moment: Day 48

Deuteronomy 10:12-13. "And now, Israel, what doth the LORD thy God require of thee, but to fear the LORD thy God, to walk in all his ways, and to love him, and to serve the LORD thy God with all thy heart and with all thy soul, to keep the commandments of the LORD, and his statutes, which I command thee this day for thy good?"

In other words, A true child of God will mirror their covenant relationships after their father. They would be faithful, they would be true, and they would keep their word. If your marriage relationship is not mirrored after your heavenly father ask him to help you to be faithful, be true and always to keep your word! Keep your covenant relationship! **Be Blessed!**

Marriage Wisdom Moment: Day 49

1 Corinthians 11:3. But I want you to understand that the head of every man is Christ, and the head of the wife is her husband, and the head of Christ is God.

In other words, this is the true order of the family. A wife cannot follow a husband who can't lead. Men of God stop complaining about what your wife does if you're not leading and she must step into your role and lead. You need to be in your proper position as the head of the house and getting your instructions from God. Not complaining about your wife whom you should be leading by example. Husbands be the example of what God has trusted you with stop letting your wife lead you. **Be Blessed!**

Marriage Wisdom Moment: Day 50

Proverbs 10:19 says: "When words are many, sin is not absent, but he who holds his tongue is wise".

In other words, let's be careful what we say and how we say things to one another that doesn't mean that you can't say anything at all. But think of words as gifts that we give to each other. Anything can also be overdone. But it can also be underdone. Ask the Lord to help you to keep wise in the balance of all that you say. Let's speak to each other in love and watch the tone in which you speak. **Be Blessed!**

Marriage Wisdom Moment: Day 51

Ecclesiastes 4:12 Says A person standing alone can be attacked and defeated, but two can stand back-to-back and conquer. Three are even better, for a triple-braided cord is not easily broken.

In other words, Put God first and keep him first in your marriage as the scripture states two are better than one and three is even better. When you have a true marriage of God, it will show. You can't serve the world in your marriage and expect it to last. Only marriages that are submitted to God will be long lasting, happy and satisfying submit your marriage to him today and see where he will take it. **Be Blessed!**

Marriage Wisdom Moment: Day 52

Matthew 12:37. But I tell you that men will have to give an account on the Day of Judgment for every careless word they have spoken. For by your words you will be acquitted, and by your words you will be condemned.

In other words, our words will hurt us or bless us. Let's be watchful of what we say to each other as husbands and wives. Our words should like big blessings we give each other every day. Don't speak something over your spouse and your marriage that you will regret. Remember what we say will come to pass. **Be Blessed!**

Date Night!
Time to Go Out!

Let's plan where you want to go and then make plans for a sitter if you have children. Take tonight to try a different restaurant or a movie you both want to see or maybe a night of bowling. Just do something you both enjoy. If you want to stay at home and have a romantic evening with takeout and a glass of wine that's fine too. Put away your cell phones and I-pads and just talk to each other. You might find that your conversation may turn romantic and then you can have each other for dessert!

Date Night Simplified!

1. Plan/Go out
2. Hire a babysitter/ if you have children
3. Try something new
4. Put away your cell phone
5. Try a romantic conversation
6. Have each other for dessert.

Marvin & Deborah's Story

When Pastor Marvin and I got married we had no clue as to what it took to succeed in marriage. We had no role models, therefore, we had no one to emulate. We did what we believed a good marriage was supposed to look like. That is a bad place to be when starting out, but we survived Thirty-Five years through God's amazing grace his grace is truly sufficient. Marriage is a choice your greatest desire should be to please God and then your spouse. It is the responsibility of each person to decide that divorce is not an option. When you decide to do whatever is necessary, then you will see the manifestation of what God had in mind when he created you.

These are the Wisdom keys to our Successful Marriage. Always seek God's will before entering a covenant with another person. Get counseling from your Pastors, a marriage counselor or someone that has a successful marriage. Make sure you understand what it means to be in a covenant relationship. Always be on one accord even when you disagree. Never invite or have unwanted guests into your marriage. Integrity, faithfulness and trust are major criteria for having a successful marriage.

Communication is a must to have a successful marriage. Always listen while the other person is talking and don't interrupt them. Never conclude without hearing the whole matter. Remember to pray about everything and your spouse. Have a forgiving heart. Allow your spouse not to be perfect and never compare them to anyone else. Always choose to love.

Find something to laugh about each day. Always keep God in the center.

Be quick to say, "I'm sorry." Remember there are no perfect marriages Again I say pray, pray, pray and pray.

These are some of the things that have kept us together. There remains a few we're still working on. If you don't acknowledge change; things will remain the same. It has and always will be God's desire for us to be successful in everything He has called us to.

Wisdom on Trust
CHAPTER 3

Marriage Wisdom Moment: Day 53

Proverbs 25:19. Confidence in an unfaithful man in a time of trouble is like a broken tooth and a foot out of joint.

In other words, be a man or woman who can be counted on in your marriage. Don't always run from every problem sit-down together and pray about what's going on and give it to God the problem solver. Remember your marriage vows says for better or worse. Don't be a spouse that run at the first sign of trouble. Be the first to get on your knees and pray your marriage through the situation this too shall pass trouble don't last forever but your marriage should. **Be Blessed!**

Marriage Wisdom Moment: Day 54

Proverbs 21:22. A wise man scales the city walls of the mighty and brings down the stronghold in which they trust.

 In other words, don't say to yourself I have money, I have a house, I have my family and don't recognize that it all came from God. Some people put their trust in all these things and think it was themselves who got them what they have. Well, you better know we serve a jealous God, and we are never to put anything or anyone before him. Thank God for all you have and don't let all you have, and your way of thinking become a stronghold trust God over all you have. **Be Blessed!**

Marriage Wisdom Moment: Day 55

Romans 4:17. As it is written, I have made you a father of many nations, before him whom he believed, even God, who gives life to the dead, and calls those things which are not as though they were.

 In other words, what are you speaking over yourself and your marriage? Do you know whatever you are saying is shaping your world? Take today to start speaking what you would like to see in your marriage and home and begin to see what happens. Our words have power so choose your words wisely whatever you need in your life start speaking those things as though they are, and it will be done. Speak in faith and God will answer. **Be Blessed!**

Marriage Wisdom Moment: Day 56

Proverbs 8:11. For wisdom is better than rubies, and all the things that may be desired are not to be compared to it.

In other words, desire wisdom in all situations instead of money or riches. Desire to know how to handle problems wisely; it's funny that people desire to be rich but don't desire the wisdom to handle the riches wow! In a marriage, we need wisdom to understand how to handle certain situations that come up. Money can't solve relationship problems, and it can't buy you love you need wisdom and God to get you through. **Be Blessed!**

Marriage Wisdom Moment: Day 57

Proverbs 27:18. Whoever keeps the fig tree will eat its fruit; so, he who waits on his master will be honored.

In other words, we need to go to God with all our problems. When we do we are seeking the kingdom first before we go and tell others about our problem. Only God can solve our problems. You need to learn how to wait on God. When we as a family are going through anything we give God at least three days to answer. It took three days for him to resurrect why do we want a microwave answer? The next time you pray about your problem give God time to answer, learn to wait for God you will never be disappointed. **Be Blessed!**

Marriage Wisdom Moment: Day 58

Deuteronomy 31:6. Be strong and courageous. Do not be afraid or terrified because of them, for the Lord your God goes with you; he will never leave you nor forsake you.

 In other words, some marriages are either coming out of something, going into something or are currently in something but whatever it is you are going through know that God is always there for you to talk to. He will never leave you nor forsake you. Pray about everything, and God will answer. He hears our prayers. **Be Blessed!**

Marriage Wisdom Moment: Day 59

Psalm 20:4 says: May he give you the desire of your heart and make all your plans succeed!

In other words, Woman of God stop looking to your husband for all your happiness. A man can't handle that much power only God can make us truly happy through our spouses. When we look to them for our happiness, they will disappoint you all the time because they don't know how to make us happy. God has made us and only he can make us happy through our spouses. Tell God what you desire in your husband or your wife and then make sure you're doing what your husband or wife desires through God. Only God can live through us to give each spouse their hearts desire. **Be Blessed!**

Marriage Wisdom Moment: Day 60

Ephesians 5:25. Husbands, love your wives, just as Christ also loved the church and gave Himself up for her.

In other words, Women need men who can cover them as the Bible says and love them; not men who allow their wives to lead, but men that can lead the family in a godly way. Men also need a wife that is beautiful on the inside and not just beautiful on the outside and who can allow a man to lead the family. If we are all in our rightful places as men and women, our homes would be in order and not out of order. God is a God of order. **Be Blessed!**

Marriage Wisdom Moment: Day 61

Mathew 19:6. So they are no longer two, but one flesh. Therefore, what God has joined together, let no one separate."

In other words, Marriages today are destroyed because of selfishness. why is it more Christians than ever getting divorces? We should be the examples if we are following the ways of Christ. Men and women of God let's wake up and see the spirit of the enemy selfishness, lying, cheating are all the ways of the enemy. Stop letting him use you against what God has put together! Stop letting others such as mother and father and other family members come between what God put together. Put God first, and your spouse second, and he will guide you to success. **Be Blessed!**

Marriage Wisdom Moment: Day 62

Proverbs 5:18-20 says: May your fountain be blessed, and may you rejoice in the wife of your youth. A loving doe, a graceful deer, may her breasts satisfy you always, may you ever be intoxicated with her love. Why, my son, be intoxicated with another man's wife? Why embrace the bosom of a wayward woman?

In other words, be happy with the wife you have and be satisfied with her breasts not the breasts of a stranger. What's blocking you from being happy in your marriage? Could it be that you're looking at someone else's spouse and relationship that seems to be happy out in the open, but they are unhappy behind closed doors? Stop building your marriage on what you think is happening and what you think their spouse is doing for them. Only build your marriage on what you know and what God has to say about it! **Be Blessed**

Marriage Wisdom Moment: Day 63

Jeremiah 29.11: For I know the plans I have for you," declares the LORD, "plans to prosper you and not to harm you, plans to give you hope and a future.

In other words, Marriage is a union set by God to bring two people together for his divine plan. Don't you owe it to yourself to find out what his plan is for your marriage? Everybody's marriage and plan are different so stop expecting your marriage to be like theirs. Pray and wait on God to show you the plans he has for your marriage. **Be Blessed!**

Marriage Wisdom Moment: Day 64

2 Corinthians 1:6. If we are afflicted, it is for your comfort and salvation, and if we are comforted, it is for your comfort, which you experience when you patiently endure the same sufferings that we suffer.

In other words, A marriage tested is a marriage that will last. Marriage is not always easy, but those are the times you can see your strengths and your weaknesses. When your marriage is tested, and you can overcome the situation and forgive then you know your marriage will last. If God is the head of your marriage he will see you through any situation there's nothing too hard for God. All storms are to strengthen you not to harm you. If you can make it through the storm that's a sign that your marriage will last and be strong. **Be Blessed!**

Marriage Wisdom Moment: Day 65

Proverbs 3:5-6. Trust in the LORD with all your heart and do not lean on your own understanding. In all your, ways acknowledge Him, and He will make your paths straight.

In other words, trust God no matter what and he will bring the situation under control. Sometimes were not trusting God in our situations and therefore we try to work it out in our own strength and it may not seem to be working. If we just learn to pray and wait and trust God, we will see that thing to the end and realize what God will was. **Be Blessed!**

Marriage Wisdom Moment: Day 66

Jeremiah 17:7-8. But blessed is the one who trusts in the Lord, whose confidence is in him. They will be like a tree planted by the water that sends out its roots by the stream. It does not fear when heat comes; its leaves are always green. It has no worries in a year of drought and never fails to bear fruit.

In other words, we ought to have confidence in the trust we have for our husbands and our wives. We should never have to worry about them doing anything that they should not be doing. There should always be honesty as well as loyalty. If you can't trust your spouse who can you trust? Pray for God to change your spouse into a trust worthy person. **Be Blessed!**

Marriage Wisdom Moment: Day 67

Psalm 56:3. When I am afraid, I put my trust in you.

In other words, we should know we can always trust God no matter what. Sometimes we are afraid of life and what it brings but we should always know he loves us and will always be there for us even when our mates are not there for us. Put all your trust in God he will never fail you. **Be Blessed!**

Marriage Wisdom Moment: Day 68

Isaiah 43:2. When you pass through the waters, I will be with you and when you pass through the rivers, they will not sweep over you. When you walk through the fire, you will not be burned; the flames will not set you ablaze.

In other words, when God is for us we never have to worry. That's how our marriages should be we should never have to worry what our spouses are saying and doing we should be able to trust them with our life. Pray for each other to be so trustworthy that you never have to worry about your spouse leaving you in a fire.
Be Blessed!

Marriage Wisdom Moment: Day 69

Psalm 143:8. Let the morning bring me word of your unfailing love, for I have put my trust in you. Show me the way I should go, for to you I entrust my life.

In other words, our lives are in God's hands. God gave us our spouses to love, honor, and trust so we should be able to trust our spouses no matter what. When you got married you made a vow to love and honor one another, well trust is in that same category. Be a spouse that can be trusted. **Be Blessed!**

Marriage Wisdom Moment: Day 70

1 John 5:14. This is the confidence we have in approaching God: that if we ask anything according to his will, he hears us

In other words, when we ask God anything in prayer according to his word which is his will he hears you so when you are praying for your spouse trust that God hears your prayers and he will answer according to his word. **Be Blessed!**

Marriage Wisdom Moment: Day 71

Psalm 91:1-2. Whoever dwells in the shelter of the Most High will rest in the shadow of the Almighty. I will say of the Lord, "He is my refuge and my fortress, my God, in whom I trust."

In other words, when we stay on our knees in our secret place praying God will abide with us and there will always a be shadow of protection we will have with God. That's the same way our trust in one another should be a shadow of protection. **Be Blessed!**

Marriage Wisdom Moment: Day 72

James 1:6. But when you ask, you must believe and not doubt, because the one who doubts is like a wave of the sea, blown and tossed by the wind.

In other words, when you ask God for anything you should trust what you asked him. You should not have any doubt that he heard and will answer you. Marriage should be the same way if your spouse told you something it should be what they said there should be no doubt what was said bottom line. **Be Blessed!**

Marriage Wisdom Moment: Day 73

Psalm 62:7. My salvation and my honor depend on God; he is my mighty rock, my refuge.

In other words, we should always depend on God for whatever we need. If we want something from our spouses go to God and trust him over your spouse to do what it is your asking if it lines up with the word of God. That's called seeking the kingdom of God first.
Be Blessed!

Marriage Wisdom Moment: Day 74

**Psalm 121:3. He will not let your foot slip
he who watches over you will not slumber.**

In other words, God will not let you fall he will be there for you no matter what. That's the way marriage should be we should be there always for one another and we should never let each other fall. Two are always better than one. **Be Blessed!**

Marriage Wisdom Moment: Day 75

Psalm 145:18. The Lord is near to all who call on him, to all who call on him in truth.

In other words, God is always there for us and all he wants is for us to live by the truth. We should always tell the truth in marriage even if it hurts. When you live in the truth you never have to worry about living a lie.
Be Blessed!

Marriage Wisdom Moment: Day 76

Proverbs 29:25. Fear of man will prove to be a snare, but whoever trusts in the Lord is kept safe

In other words, it's always wise to trust God in whatever situation you may find yourself in because God will keep us safe. If our spouses are not being trustworthy we need to take them to prayer and trust God over them. He has a way of changing the heart of your spouse. **Be Blessed!**

Date Night!
It's Your Night!

Do something fun tonight for one another make this date about the other. If it's the husband's night then, wife do something he likes such as going to a game or changing your bed spread or comforter to his favorite team logos for the night. How about going to a sports bar to watch the game and eat or if he like pool or darts maybe you should take him there to enjoy himself or maybe just take him to his favorite spot.

Just remember this night is about the other person. Ok husbands if you are choosing this date to be special for your wife then make an appointment for a massage for both of you at her favorite spa. Maybe take her to her favorite nail salon, and you be patient while she's being pampered or take her to a romantic movie or just to her favorite place. Just remember to make it fun for both of you even though it's about the other person tonight.

Date Night Simplified!

1. This date is about the other person
2. Plan who it's about and what you're going to do (planning is a must)
3. Make it fun and enjoyable for both of you
4. Remember it's about the other person tonight your turn is coming

De Carlo and Marian's Story

Twenty-seven years ago, we stood before God and many witnesses repeating the vows of love, commitment and dedication to one another. It was a day that has been indelibly etched in our hearts and minds. As we continue to grow in our relationship as husband and wife, we've learned that the key to a successful marriage is keeping Christ in the center of our relationship. Every new day brings even greater love, excitement and contentment. When we follow God's prescription for marriage it will endure every test, trial or storm.

Every relationship will be tested whether it's a friendship or marriage it will undergo pressure, but the good news is that with the right information and the wisdom to appropriately apply it, our relationships will become stronger enabling us to endure any trial.

The Bible declares in Ephesians 5:25 Husbands, love your wives even as Christ also loved the church, and gave Himself for it this is one of my favorite marriage scriptures because it speaks to men on so many levels; it speaks to single men who will one day marry, and it speaks to married men.

It communicates the fidelity and great love that Christ has for the church, His caring and tireless commitment for its establishment and continued development. He then ultimately demonstrates His love by His willingness to lay down His life for it. As men we are called to be a priest in our homes, loving, strengthening, encouraging and sacrificially giving of ourselves, building up our wives that they may fulfill their potential and destiny.

WISDOM ON RESPECT
CHAPTER 4

Marriage Wisdom Moment: Day 77

Ephesians 5:33. So again I say; each man must love his wife as he loves himself, and the wife must respect her husband.

In other words, you can't keep putting your husband or wife down and then expect them to respect and love you later it just doesn't work that way. Complement them and tell them what they are doing right instead of what they are doing wrong. You will get further doing that than always putting them down for what you believe they can't do. Love your spouse where they are. **Be Blessed!**

Marriage Wisdom Moment: Day 78

Ephesians 5:22. Wives submit yourselves unto your own husbands as unto the Lord.

In other words, Wives sometimes don't want to submit to our husbands because we think they will walk all over us but let us respect them enough to do what they ask. Trust God over him and his attitude God will judge his actions. If it's something, you're not comfortable with then pray that God will lead you both. **Be Blessed!**

Marriage Wisdom Moment: Day 79

Genesis 2:18. And the Lord God said it is not good that the man should be alone I will make a helper for him.

In other words, women of God, we are to be our husband's helper, not his mother and not his boss. We are to talk to him with respect and treat him like our husbands. If we learn how to communicate with him then, we will know how to help him in the way God intended. If you don't know ask God to show you how. Remember he knows your husband better than you. **Be Blessed!**

Marriage Wisdom Moment: Day 80

Proverbs 20:19. He who goes about as a talebearer reveals secrets; therefore associate, not with him talks too freely.

In other words, as a married couple you must be very careful who you share your marital business with. Everybody don't have your best interest at heart. The person you might be trusting could be telling your business to someone you don't like or trust. If you truly need to talk to someone make sure, they are God approved like your pastor or elder in the church. If you don't go to church, then talk to God yourself and ask him to change your situation. Trust the Lord Jesus Christ only with your marriage and ask his direction, and he will direct you to someone who is God approved. **Be Blessed!**

Marriage Wisdom Moment: Day 81

Proverbs 3:5 says: Trust in the LORD with all your heart and lean not on your own understanding;

In other words, sometimes as husbands and wives we put our happiness in one another and trust, and when that person isn't making us happy any more, we blame them and then we want a divorce. Well, we should never put all our happiness and trust into our mates we should be putting all our happiness and trust in God, who can handle it. Our mates can't handle that much power besides only God can make you happy through your mate. Take today to trust God over your happiness, and he will make you happy through your mate. Only God knows. **Be Blessed!**

Marriage Wisdom Moment: 82

Proverbs 27:17. As iron sharpens iron, so one person sharpens another.

In other words, we as children of God help each other become better. So as husbands and wives we should be helping each other all the time become better. Sometimes were doing things that irritate one another but we should always be open with our spouses to tell them what were irritated about. The problem is how and when we choose to tell the other person. We should never be angry or judgmental, we should tell them in a way that would help them fix the problem in a better way and be better at it. Pray for God's timing when dealing with sensitive issues concerning your spouse. **Be Blessed!**

Marriage Wisdom Moment: Day 83

Proverbs 11:22. Like a gold ring and a pig's snout is a beautiful woman who shows no discretion.

In other words, we as women should have a better perspective about ourselves, once we get married unto the Lord as well as to our husbands. We should not be dressing with everything showing letting all the world see what only your husband should see. We also shouldn't be loud and belligerent and embarrassing and wonder why our husbands don't want to go anywhere with us.

Once you taste and see how good the Lord is you should be changing and growing. I hear women all the time talking about they want husbands. Well I say this start learning how a wife should conduct herself first and then ask God to send you a husband and he will. Show some respect to your husband by showing some discretion and respect for yourself! **Be Blessed!**

Marriage Wisdom Moment: Day 84

Proverbs 17:16. Why should fools have money in hand to buy wisdom; when they are not able to understand?

In other words, money can't buy wisdom; wisdom is learned and understood. If you never go through anything as a married couple how can you gain wisdom to help someone else. I know a lot of time we wish we had lots of money for this or that, but money can't buy everything. Sometimes you will have to experience some things and come out of it victoriously and gain the wisdom needed to show someone else how to come through. Don't be a fool with money trying to buy wisdom you can't buy it. You must experience it to understand. **Be Blessed!**

Marriage Wisdom Moment: Day 85

Philippians 2:3-4. Do nothing from rivalry or conceit, but in humility count others more significant than yourselves. Let each of you look not only to his own interests, but also to the interests of others.

In other words, what you respect you will attract. Do you respect your husband or your wife? Do you respect your money, or the job God has provided you? Do you respect your friends or people God is putting in your path? What you respect you will attract. Start respecting what God has given you, and the people he put in your life and he will give you more. **Be Blessed!**

Marriage Wisdom Moment: Day 86

2 Corinthians 5:10. For we must all appear before the judgment seat of Christ, so that each of us may receive what is due us for the things done while in the body, whether good or bad.

In other words, the key to a long-lasting marriage is to stop trying to change the other person. Just love that person for who they are and where they are and accept them the way they are. Pray for God to make you both one and accept the challenges that come your way. Remember whatever he or she is lacking you make it up as their spouse that's what make you one in the first place! **Be Blessed!**

Marriage Wisdom Moment: Day 87

Proverbs 18:21 says: The tongue has the power of life and death, and those who love it will eat its fruit.

In other words, Life and death are in the power of your tongue speak life over your marriage, and life will happen. Speak happiness over your marriage, and it will happen, speak love and blessings, and that also will happen, speak divorce and infidelity, hate and anger and those things will happen too. Speak what you want, and you shall have it! **Be Blessed!**

Marriage Wisdom Moment: Day 88

Luke 6:31. Treat others the same way you want them to treat you.

In other words, Marriage is a covenant before God, and we should treat it as such, so when we decide to treat our spouses any kind of way just know that you are doing the same to God and before God. Remember God is watching everything we do so let's treat our spouse like we would have them treat us. **Be Blessed!**

Marriage Wisdom Moment: Day 89

Psalm 37:5. Commit everything you do to the LORD. Trust him, and he will help you.

In other words, commit your ways and the ways of your marriage to God and he shall establish your path. When you invite God to be the head of your marriage it will last way past any problems you might have. Remember he is a way maker and he is a strong tower let him strengthen your marriage and direct its path. **Be Blessed!**

Marriage Wisdom Moment: Day 90

Colossians 3:9-11. Do not lie to one another, since you laid aside the old self with its evil practices,

In other words, once you give your life to the Lord you should not be still telling lies. The old self should be gone and now you should be aware that God sees and hears everything we do. It should be the same in marriage if you were mature enough to get married you should not lie only immature people have to tell lies. **Be Blessed!**

Marriage Wisdom Moment: Day 91

Proverbs 28:21. To show partiality is not good, because for a piece of bread a man will transgress

In other words, we should never show more love to one kind of person and no love towards another kind of person. God don't want us treating anyone else better than we treat others don't you know that is a lie too. It's deceptive because the other people don't know how your treating them. Love everyone and especially your spouse in truth.

Marriage Wisdom Moment: Day 92

1 Peter 2:17. Honor all people, love the brotherhood, fear God, honor the king.

In other words, love other's as you love yourself and respect those in authority. In your marriage your husband is in authority over your marriage and family, so make sure you choose the right authority over you and your marriage. Sometime our husbands are not leading the way they should. If that's your issue, then take your husband to prayer and ask God to change his heart to want to take his position as the authority in your home serious and God will hear and begin to make those changes. **Be Blessed!**

Marriage Wisdom Moment: Day 93

Colossians 3:18-19. Wives, be subject to your husbands, as is fitting in the Lord.

In other words, ladies respect your husband's authority and respect it enough to do what they ask. If they are not leading like they should take them to God in prayer and ask God to change their heart, but if your husband is subject to God then you as the wife should do what is asked. Don't expect your husband to be mature in God if you married a man who knows nothing about God. The bible says don't agree with someone who is not on the same path as you. **Be Blessed!**

Marriage Wisdom Moment: Day 94

1 Peter 3:6-7. just as Sarah obeyed Abraham, calling him lord, and you have become her children if you do what is right without being frightened by any fear.

In other words, you should always be in a loving relationship there should never be any fear. If your loving your spouse and doing right by them then there should be no problem. If you married an abusive man GET OUT NOW! You can't pray for an abusive man to change especially if he's beating you. If you want, you can pray for them to change but do it from a distance. Abuse is NEVER OK! **Be Blessed!**

Marriage Wisdom Moment: Day 95

Deuteronomy 1:13-15. 'Choose wise and discerning and experienced men from your tribes, and I will appoint them as your heads.'

In other words, when you say you want to marry a man of God make sure that's what he is. Don't be deceived by how is in the beginning. Always take every situation to prayer so God can reveal the truth about this person your about get involved with or get married too. You wouldn't buy a house without checking it out, first would you? Take the time to pray and make sure your choosing the right authority over your life. Remember you will be married until death do you part. **Be Blessed!**

Marriage Wisdom Moment: Day 96

Proverbs 31:23. Her husband is known in the gates, when he sits among the elders of the land.

In other words, your spouse should have so much integrity that he is known amongst his peers as a loving and kind person. If the peers of the man your looking to get married to is telling you all sorts of bad things about this man those are warnings from God not to get involved with him. God gives us warnings before we make any major decisions in life and marriage is a big decision. Pray and let God reveal the truth. **Be Blessed!**

Marriage Wisdom Moment: Day 97

1 Timothy 3:2-11. An overseer, then, must be above reproach, the husband of one wife, temperate, prudent, respectable, hospitable, able to teach,

In other words, your husband is the overseer of your marriage, family, and home and he should not be having no affairs, he should be a man of integrity. You as a wife should be learning something from your husband all the time. He should be leading by example therefore teaching the right things to you and your children. If that's not the case, take your husband to God in prayer and ask him to change your husband heart to desire to lead by example. **Be Blessed!**

Marriage Wisdom Moment: Day 98

Romans 13:1-7. Every person is to be in subjection to the governing authorities for there is no authority except from God, and those which exist are established by God.

In other words, we should respect those who are in authority because God put them in place. No matter where that authority exists we should be respecting them as such. We may not always like what our spouses say or do but we should respect them for who they are. We should be respecting our bosses at work and those we meet daily who are in a position of authority. It's not what you think they should be doing but who God put in place. **Be Blessed!**

Marriage Wisdom Moment: Day 99

1 Thessalonians 5:12. But we request of you, brethren, that you appreciate those who diligently labor among you, and have charge over you in the Lord and give you instruction,

In other words, God gave you your job and you should be respecting your boss. You should never take anything for granted. Stop complaining about your boss, your spouse and or your children. God put your boss in that position and he put your spouse in that position so pray about it. **Be Blessed!**

Marriage Wisdom Moment: Day 100

Hebrews 13:17. Obey your leaders and submit to them, for they keep watch over your souls as those who will give an account. Let them do this with joy and not with grief, for this would be unprofitable for you.

In other words, when we are married our husbands are our protectors and so with that being said let them protect you and stop giving them grief for doing their job. You should thank God when your husband warns you against doing certain things especially if your husband is a man of God. He is just doing what God intended for him to do. He wants to keep you safe and he's showing you he loves you.

Be Blessed!

Marriage Wisdom Moment: Day 101

1 Timothy 5:1-2. Do not sharply rebuke an older man, but rather appeal to him as a father, to the younger men as brothers,

In other words, we should be respecting each other even if we don't think we should. Sometimes in marriage we lose respect for each other because of what we see with each other's daily habits and that begins to unravel the marriage. We should always keep that respect level no matter what we know about our spouses. God wants us to be respectful no matter what. **Be Blessed!**

Marriage Wisdom Moment: Day 102

Philippians 2:3 Do nothing from selfishness or empty conceit, but with humility of mind let each of you regard one another as more important than himself;

In other words, let's choose to make your spouse and your marriage your priority. If there is no marriage, there is no family. Sometimes were doing so much that were putting everything above our spouses and our marriages. If you put nothing into your marriage you can't expect to get anything out of it. Make your marriage a priority.
Be Blessed!

Date Night
Quality Time!

Don't you know quality time is not about quantity time? Quality planning is the best thing you can do in your marriage. How about an intimate date night full of just talking about your lives and future together? How about a beautiful picnic in the park if it's warm out? What about a picnic in your bedroom with the fireplace on. Set up a small table for two with a bottle of wine or champagne or apple cider whatever you prefer and just enjoy each other's time. Looking into each other eyes and just speaking what comes to mind about each other. Intimacy is not all about sex but if what you are saying leads to it then that's the icing on the cake.

Date Night Simplified!

1. Quality over quantity
2. Planning is a must
3. Be creative with ideas and weather changes
4. Try intimacy without sex at first
5. Enjoy each other's time

William & Loretta's Story

In our relationship respect is something we found hard to do the more we got to know each other. Sometimes in marriage you feel you get to know your spouse so well that you no longer feel you need to show them respect, but you do. One thing we have learned about respect is that it's earned not just given. When you show respect for your spouse, they will automatically show respect to you.

The bible says you reap what you sow. Like I said earlier, I was very disrespectful in my ways and my speaking to my husband, and he was disrespectful in return. You see how it works both in disrespect and respect? God showed me my wicked ways by saying to me "How Dare You Speak to Him That Way! That Is My Son. That stopped me right there, and God began to show me how to respect him. You see there was no respect for men in my family I have always seen the women dominate the man, so I thought that was what I was supposed to do.

I wanted to be in control all the time. I would use things I knew about my husband to my advantage like sex or use the divorce word to get my way. I would put him down and talk to him crazy, But God showed me what was right. I was what it said in **Proverbs 21:9. Better to live on a corner of the roof than share a house with a quarrelsome wife**. Yes, that was truly me. I was so mean and hateful towards my husband and I now know that it was my examples that were in front of me as well as the sexual abuse I endured. Everything was fueled by anger.

I was in a dark place in the beginning years of our marriage.

Thank you, Lord, for deliverance and being set free. I now thank God for my husband I truly respect him and love him with my whole heart. God through my husband has taught me how to love and how to care and respect him. You see being respectful doesn't mean you're a door mat for your spouse just trust the God in your spouse to love and respect you the way God would have him to do.

WISDOM ON FINANCES
CHAPTER 5
Marriage Wisdom Moment: Day 103

Proverbs 3:9. Honor the Lord with your capital sufficiency and the first fruits of all your income, so shall your storage places be filled with plenty and your vats shall be overflowing with new wine.

In other words, if you are struggling financially in your marriage here is a plan to stop struggling. Agree to give to the kingdom of God together on one accord and watch God turn your finances around. Watch lack just disappear because you chose God's financial plan to give instead of the world financial plan of hoarding (keeping). Pray together and ask God where to give and how much and follow his lead. **Be Blessed!**

Marriage Wisdom Moment: Day 104

Proverbs 17:16. Of what use is money in the hand of a fool to buy skillful and godly wisdom when he has no understanding or heart for it.

In other words, why let the one who has no understanding about how to budget and use the money wisely handle the finances in your marriage. If you are always struggling to pay this and that could it be that the one doing the household budget is a fool when it comes to handling the money? Everybody don't have the gift of budgeting, so if your spouse is better handling the money than you then trust the God in them to handle the budget, and the struggle will be removed. **Be Blessed!**

Marriage Wisdom Moment: Day 105

Proverbs 22:1. A good name is to be chosen rather than great riches, loving favor rather than silver and gold.

In other words, if God has been showing you favor in your marriage, family and job then don't let family members or other people cause you to move from where you are being blessed to where you may have a struggle.

Sometimes God will call your family out from your other family members and some friend's, so he can do the work in you and in the process of your obedience he gives you favor in your family and finances. Remember the enemy will try to use someone you love to get you out of place of your blessing, so you can struggle. Be careful who you are following and listening to. God is the only one who should have the last say in our lives not people only God can change your situation. **Be Blessed!**

Marriage Wisdom Moment: Day 106

Proverbs 16:8. Better is a little with righteousness than great income with injustice.

In other words, it's better to have a little money with peace than a whole lot of money with fighting. I think it's so funny that when you first start out in marriage and you have little money you seem to get along good, but the minute you are making more money that's when fighting and arguing step in. Let's be content and happy with money as well as without. Money should not be the center of your happiness God should be. **Be Blessed!**

Marriage Wisdom Moment: Day 107

Proverbs 13:11. Wealth obtained by fraud dwindles, but the one who gathers by labor increases it.

In other words, money gotten by robbing or cheating someone will be lost fast but the one who works honestly for the money it will last. We as married couples should not be defrauding anyone don't you know God is watching what you are doing to get money as well as what you are doing with the money? When we cheat someone out of money someone will ultimately cheat you also. Let's make our money by God's standard and let him lead you to great and mighty riches. He is the only one who know the plans he has for you. **Be Blessed!**

Marriage Wisdom Moment: Day 109

Luke 16:10. He who is faithful in a very little thing is faithful also in much; and he who is unrighteous in a very little thing is unrighteous also in much.

In other words, if you are not faithful to God in the little he asks you to give then you will not be faithful if he gave you a lot. Stop telling God when you make a lot of money you will start giving NO! God is looking for you to start giving out of your little, so he can be the one to bless you with a lot. If you won't do it now, you really won't do it later. Give and watch God do great and mighty things. **Be Blessed!**

Marriage Wisdom Moment: Day 110

1 Timothy 5:18 For the Scripture says, "Do not muzzle the ox while it is treading out the grain," and "The worker deserves his wages."

In other words, don't tie down a person when they are doing something good and give a person what they deserve. When we are married sometimes our spouses can work so much that they don't have a balance. Too many times I have seen spouses go and find someone else to spend time with because their spouse is working a lot.

Don't do that your spouse is working hard for you and your family. If this is your situation pray for balance for your spouse, so they don't lose sight of what God has blessed them with. Don't go adding more problems be that faithful spouse and reward them for being awesome providers pray instead for balance God will change it. **Be Blessed!**

Marriage Wisdom Moment: Day 111

James 5:4. Look! The wages you failed to pay the workmen who mowed your fields are crying out against you. The cries of the harvesters have reached the ears of the Lord Almighty.

In other words, pay those you owe. The bible tells us to owe no man but to love them. We as married couples shouldn't hire people to do things for us and then we want to find a way not to pay them. Stop also paying some of your bills and not all and end up in more debt because you're living in partiality (partly) paying your bills. If God has blessed you with income pay who you owe, it is a sin to live in overage! **Be Blessed!**

Marriage Wisdom Moment: Day 112

Matthew 6:31-33. "Do not worry then, saying, 'What will we eat?' or 'What will we drink?' or 'What will we wear for clothing?' "For the Gentiles eagerly seek all these things; for your heavenly Father knows that you need all these things. "But seek first His kingdom and His righteousness, and all these things will be added to you.

In other words, why are you worrying about things that God can provide? As married couples we need to seek God for everything. There should never be a problem with anything we need if God is the head of your marriage. It's God who supplies all your needs no matter what they are. Remember the earth is the Lords and the fullness there of. Don't you belong to him too? **Be Blessed!**

Marriage Wisdom Moment: Day 113

Philippians 4:11-13. For I have learned to be content, whatever the circumstances may be. I know now how to live when things are difficult, and I know how to live when things are prosperous. In general, and I have learned the secret of eating well or going hungry of facing either plenty of poverty. I am ready for anything through the strength of the One who lives within me.

In other words, we should be so confident in the Lord that we are content in any situation no matter what it is. God should be the head of your life and your marriage and that is the secret to being content. If we are seeking God and his Kingdom first then, there should be nothing we have need of in any situation because we should have confidence that he will provide what we need. **Be Blessed!**

Marriage Wisdom Moment: Day 114

1 Timothy 6:7-10. For we brought nothing into the world, and we can take nothing out of it. But if we have food and clothing, we will be content with that. People who want to get rich fall into temptation and a trap and into many foolish and harmful desires that plunge men into ruin and destruction. For the love of money is a root of all kinds of evil. Some people, eager for money, have wandered from the faith and pierced themselves with many griefs.

In other words, let's learn to be to be content with the income God has provided for you. Let's not run after money which can cause all kinds of trouble by you doing corrupt things to get it. God did not intend for us as married couples to make money by over working.

Sometimes were working way too many hours and too many days trying to make ends meet? Don't you know by giving and trusting God over your finances more that God can increase your finances in ways you never thought he could. Trust God more and give more and cut back on work and give your marriage and family more attention and watch God work on your behalf.
Be Blessed!

Marriage Wisdom Moment: Day 115

Deuteronomy 15:6. For the Lord your God will bless you as He has promised you, and you will lend to many nations, but you will not borrow; and you will rule over many nations, but they will not rule over you.

In other words, God doesn't want us to borrow. Sometimes in marriage you get into a rut and you need a little help and that's ok, but when you need a little help every month then that's a problem. If ends are not meeting then, you need a monthly budget, so you can see what's going out verses what's coming in. If you have more going out then coming in then, you need to cut some expenses. Ask God to guide you he will. **Be Blessed!**

Marriage Wisdom Moment: Day 116

Deuteronomy 15:10. Give generously to him and do so without a grudging heart; then because of this the Lord your God will bless you in all your work and in everything you put your hand to.

In other words, when God asks you as a married couple to give, do it on one accord and because God said so. When God gives you directional giving, he will bless you beyond measure. When God directs your giving, you will never want for anything else. Try God and his plan for giving you will never be disappointed! **Be Blessed!**

Marriage Wisdom Moment: Day 117

Proverbs 11:24-25. There is one who scatters, and yet increases more, and there is one who withholds what is justly due, and yet it results only in want. The generous man will be prosperous, and he who waters will himself be watered.

In other words, Put Giving first in your finances and allow God to give you more in return. When we hold what God has told us to give we live under a closed heaven, and suddenly you are struggling to make ends meet. When you give generously, it will return to you generously. Trust God over your finances! **Be Blessed!**

Marriage Wisdom Moment: Day 118

Luke 6:38 Give, and it will be given to you. They will pour into your lap a good measure, pressed down, shaken together, and running over. For by your standard of measure it will be measured to you in return.

In other words, if you give, more will be given back to you. The same amount you give to God he will give it back to you it's just that simple. As a married couple God wants us to be in agreement when giving. He does not want to divide our homes on this issue. He wants to give us our hearts desires, but we just need to trust him with what he has given us. **Be Blessed!**

Marriage Wisdom Moment: Day 119

Proverbs 13:16. A wise man thinks ahead; a fool doesn't, and even brags about it!

In other words, plan and don't be a fool who don't plan and then brag about it. In marriage there should be a plan to succeed the bible says where there is no vision the people perish. It's funny how you can plan to succeed financially but not plan to have longevity in your marriage. If you put nothing into your marriage don't expect to get anything out! **Be Blessed!**

Marriage Wisdom Moment: Day 120

Luke 12:42-44. And the Lord said, "Who then is the faithful and sensible steward, whom his master will put in charge of his servants, to give them their rations at the proper time? "Blessed is that slave whom his master finds so doing when he comes. "Truly I say to you that he will put him in charge of all his possessions.

In other words, as a married couple are you being good stewards of what God has trusted you with? God is a god of order and if you are not being a good steward over what he has trusted you with he can't give you more. If you want more from the Kingdom, then you need to be able to handle more bottom line. **Be Blessed!**

Marriage Wisdom Moment: Day 121

Nehemiah 2:20." The God of heaven will give us success; therefore, we His servants will arise and build…"

In other words. God gives us success to build his kingdom. It's for us as married couples to use the resources God has trusted us with to glorify him not to brag and promote ourselves. Make sure when success comes your way you give God all the praise and the honor for it because it all belongs to him. **Be Blessed!**

Marriage Wisdom Moment: Day 122

Proverbs 22:7 says: The rich rules over the poor and the borrower is the slave of the lender.

In other words, stop living like a borrower and start living like a lender. It's time to start living with in your means and stop borrowing. What you need to do is start saving so that you have money to lend. Live by the eighty twenty rules, which is give 10% and save that same 10% and live off the rest that way you begin saving money to lend. **Be Blessed!**

Date Night!
One Night Stand!

How about one-night stand with your spouse. Call up your family members to see who can babysit then run a hot bath put candles around the tub. Turn on some romantic music. Use a trail of flowers that lead to the bath. Use aromatherapy scents in the water plan to bathe together and then have a glass of whatever you enjoy drinking. Just soak together and let your mind indulge in each other's presence and let love lead the way!

Date Night Simplified!

1. Get a sitter if you have children
2. Plan a hot bath with aromatherapy and candles
3. Put on some romantic music
4. Use a flower trail from the front door to the bath
5. Bathe together and have a glass of whatever you like to drink
6. Let love lead the way.

Herb & Sharon's Story

Growing up I watched my parents' marriage relationship and decided that marriage would not be a part of the equation for my life. My parents were great as parents and provided a great platform for me to succeed in life. They provided the best of everything they could give... education, classical training, religious studies and great work ethics, etc.... It was important to them that I was a sound thinker and secured enough to evaluate situations correctly to become a productive, useful strong-minded citizen. As loving, caring and providing as my parents were their training also provided me with the tools to analyze their relationship and say, "No Thank You," to marriage!

As I entered my college years, I was very determined and committed to never getting married. My goal was simple, get educated, and make great career choices. In the interim, I met and fell in love with "My Knight in Shining Armor, Herb." There was immediate chemistry and connection, my philosophy on life and marriage, just thrown out the window! Herb had a loving mother but was predominately raised by his dad who was married five times...yes, I said five times. Herb's parents divorced early on, so his summation of a healthy marriage was skewed.

Herb's dad was a driven self-made millionaire early on in life. His gaze was mainly financially focused. Love to him meant, I'll provide the best of everything for my children. Emotional security, Herb was left on his own. It's very interesting sitting back logging a collection of interesting facts that lead up to the success and almost failure of our now thirty-year marriage.

Often while reading the scriptures, I remind myself that these were accounts lived out on the stage of human history by men and women like you and me. They too had to learn how to navigate in life though yielding, trial and error experiences and sometimes just mere, simple observations. Habakkuk 2: as our passion grew for each other, our knowledge and revelation of truth in this area stayed the same, minimal. The church I attended at the time was so engulfed in outer appearances that it looked like nobody needed help, but us! For years, Herb and I were essentially on our own.

Through much trial and error, I finally nerved myself enough to ask a woman I highly respected what she thought about submission. The big "S" word. She asks me what I thought. I stated to her that I hated it. Are you surprised I stated it so emphatically? Most women think like this they let the enemies lies blind them. She smiled and said to me sweetheart; I don't always like it either. It's not based on your feelings it's based on the fact that we trust God enough to know that He's not got our back! That was the beginning finally, of moving in the right direction. Somehow, I thought it meant I couldn't think, dream, move, cry or make decisions without permission from my husband.

By the leading of the Holy Spirit, Herb and I begin to study and meditate on The Grace of God. The Grace of God flowing in our lives meant that we were not our own or on our own. We belonged to another, Jesus Christ. He who created both of us knew how to reach our hearts without pressure from the other party. We finally realized that if God was gently caring and teaching us as individuals what right did we have to put such dark, scrutinizing pressures on each other in the quest for happiness. It's never perfect situations that keep us its God's presence alone. As we began to love on each other through God's eyes instead of trying to fix each other, we began to take strides in our relationship. **Phil. 4:11 tells us to be content in every situation.** It doesn't say you'll be content when your mate is in order. A yielded to Him life keeps the flow sweet. I don't know the last time submission was used as a weapon.

The weapons of our warfare are not of the flesh but have divine power to destroy strongholds, and every lofty OPINION by raising high the word, instead of lashing out insults and ultimatums. We love, enjoy and respect each other now more than ever! The love of God draws us to change our minds concerning a thing, not scripture bashing. Manipulation is never a good tool to stir one another up to do good. As husband and wife, we are on the same team, sometimes different positions, but never the less on the same side. Study one another Heb.10:24-25 learn how to be your mate's biggest fan. Let the enemy know, you're No Longer Welcome Here by unconditionally loving one another.

WISDOM ON SEX
CHAPTER 6

Marriage Wisdom Moment: Day 123

Proverbs 6:32. But whoever commits adultery with a woman lacks heart and understanding, he who does it is destroying his own life.

In other words, adultery is a choice not something that just happens so if you are making this choice you lack understanding. The Bible says you destroy your own life and family when you do it. Remember adultery is premeditated so no excuses, if you are thinking of doing it Stop and Repent! Ask God to keep you from sin and he will. **Be Blessed!**

Marriage Wisdom Moment: Day 124

1 Corinthians 7:1-40 says: Now concerning the matters about which you wrote: "It is good for a man not to have sexual relations with a woman." But because of the temptation to sexual immorality, each man should have his own wife and each woman her own husband. The husband should give to his wife her conjugal rights, and likewise the wife to her husband. For the wife does not have authority over her own body, but the husband does. Likewise, the husband does not have authority over his own body, but the wife does. Do not deprive one another, except perhaps by agreement for a limited time, that you may devote yourselves to prayer, but then come together again, so that Satan may not tempt you because of your lack of self-control.

In other words, don't holdout sexually on your husband or wife even if you're mad. The word of God clearly states that the devil will tempt you for your inconsistency with one another. Sex is a very important part of the marriage, and we should be enjoying it the way God intended don't let the devil cause you to be inconsistent and tempted. **Be Blessed!**

Marriage Wisdom Moment: Day 125

Proverbs 7:25. Let not your heart inclined toward her ways (ways of a harlot), do not stray into her paths.

In other words, men of God stop falling for the oldest trick in the book adultery! All that harlot wants to do is to destroy your anointing and your reputation as a man of God and destroy your marriage and family. Always dwell in your secret place (Psalms 91), and God will make known when a harlot tries to show up, so you will stand in temptation. Women of God keep your husband before the Lord. **Be Blessed!**

Marriage Wisdom Moment: Day 124

Proverbs 30:20. This is the way of an adulterous woman; she eats and wipes her mouth and says I have done no wickedness.

In other words, when a woman is in an adulterous affair she feels she's right and has done nothing wrong. Well, the bible clearly tells you that adultery is wicked. I don't care what you feel your husband is not doing an affair is wrong! Whatever you feel your husband is not doing ask and seek God for it instead of being in adultery. Many times, and affair comes from being selfish and from having a lack of respect for your husband. Maybe the problem you feel you are having is in you and not your husband. Ask God to show you what your problem is and once he does correct it, repent of it and be grateful and thankful for your husband. **Be Blessed!**

Marriage Wisdom Moment: Day 125

1Corinthians 7:2. But because of the temptation to sexual immorality, each man should have his own wife and each woman her own husband. Don't you know that you must put quality time in your marriage?

In other words, if you don't put anything into your marriage don't expect to get anything out of it. God made marriage for us to enjoy, and sometimes we let all these outside influences in our lives to take us away from what should be most important our marriage. It's funny how we will spend all this time at work or with our friends or going here and there, but give your marriage only minimal time and expected to work think about it? **Be Blessed!**

Marriage Wisdom Moment: Day 126

Genesis 2:24. Therefore, a man shall leave his father and his mother and hold fast to his wife, and they shall become one flesh.

In other words, men of God, you need to know that your mother does not come before your wife. The bible clearly says that you are to leave your parents and cleave to your wife. There are so many marriages today failing because mothers' in-laws keep coming in between their son and his marriage. Men of God it's time to stand up and take your rightful place, God is first and then your wife and children not your mother. It's time to be the man God called you to be and the priest of your home. **Be Blessed!**

Marriage Wisdom Moment: Day 127

Matthew 5:28. But I say to you that everyone who looks at a woman with lustful intent has already committed adultery with her in his heart.

In other words, if you are a married man or woman you have no business flirting or even looking at another woman or man in a lustful way. If you are doing this, you already in the eyes of God are committing adultery. God see's all things, you may think you're getting away with it now because you haven't been caught, but God will deal with you in the end. God will not be mocked you will reap the consequences of your actions. Repent and turn from it while you still have a chance! **Be Blessed!**

Marriage Wisdom Moment: Day 128

1 Corinthians 6:16. Or do you not know that he who is joined to a prostitute becomes one body with her? For, as it is written, "The two will become one flesh."

In other words, if you are married and are sleeping around on your spouse you are now joined as one flesh with those people. It is so important to be faithful in your marriage because you do become one spiritually with your spouse when you make love. That's why we are to have a spouse and not just be out there sleeping with this one or that one. Don't you know the value of one? There's nothing like being with that one person that God was kind enough to design just for you. Stop taking your life and your family for granted enjoy and be faithful to whom God designed just for you. **Be Blessed!**

Marriage Wisdom Moment: Day 129

Hebrews 13:4 Let marriage be held in honor among all, and let the marriage bed be undefiled, for God will judge the sexually immoral and adulterous.

In other words, when you are married you and your spouse can explore many things sexually if you both are in agreement with it. Other people should not be allowed in your bedroom such as threesomes unless it's the holy spirit. If you and your spouse are one, then you adding another person is sin. **Be Blessed!**

Marriage Wisdom Moment: Day 130

Song of Solomon 1:2. Let him kiss me with kisses of his mouth for thy love is better than wine.

In other words, kissing and hugging should happen daily in your marriage. We as married couples should always be touching and loving one another because it lets our spouses know not only do we love and want them, but that they are important to us just like God intended for them to be. **Be Blessed!**

Marriage Wisdom Moment: Day 131

**Song of Solomon 7:6-7 How beautiful and pleasant
you are, O loved one, with all your delights
Your stature is like a palm tree,
and your breasts are like its clusters.**

In other words, be in love with the breasts and body of your own spouse. Love what you see and express that to them. Let your spouse know you love how God designed their body and how much you love what they have. This will keep your mind on your own spouse and not on someone else's. God designed your spouse's body for your enjoyment. **Be Blessed**

Marriage Wisdom Moment: Day 132

**Song of Solomon 7:8-9 say I will climb the palm tree and lay hold of its fruit. Oh, may your breasts be like clusters of the vine,
and the scent of your breath like apples,
and your mouth like the best wine.**

In other words, have sex talk with your spouse and let them know how you feel about them. Describe how they look to you and let them know what you would like to do to them in the bedroom. Let what's in your heart flow out to your spouse. God blessed you with your spouse so speak your heart desires. **Be Blessed!**

Marriage Wisdom Moment: Day 133

Song of Solomon 7: 10-11. I am my beloved's, and his desire is for me. Come, my beloved, let us go out into the fields and lodge in the villages;

In other words, desire your own wife or husband and let your desire be for them only. Making love should be exciting and satisfying. Making time and making love to each other should never be boring. Role play sometimes with each other like making a date and pretending not to know each other or playing doctor and nurse. Make loving each other fun and be willing to fulfill each other's desires. God would love that. **Be Blessed!**

Marriage Wisdom Moment: Day 134

Ephesians 5:3. 3 But among you there must not be even a hint of sexual immorality, or of any kind of impurity, or of greed, because these are improper for God's holy people.

In other words, if you call yourself a man or woman of God you should **NOT!** be found in an adulterous relationship. God is saying this is not proper behavior especially if you say you have a relationship with him. When we love God, we should represent him with integrity and loyalty.
Be Blessed!

Marriage Wisdom Moment: Day 135

Galatians 5:19. 19 The acts of the flesh are obvious: sexual immorality, impurity and debauchery;

In other words, when you change your life over to Christ you should not still be living in the old way. When we give our lives to God we should be living a new life unto him. The flesh still can be tempted but after having your mind renewed and as you grow in the faith the old you should pass away all together. When you are married you are no longer single, so you shouldn't be out there living like you are single by sleeping around with this or that. When you make a vow, it is until death do you part. **Be Blessed!**

Marriage Wisdom Moment: Day 136

Mark 7:22-23. 22 adultery, greed, malice, deceit, lewdness, envy, slander, arrogance and folly. All these evils come from inside and defile a person."

In other words, when you are evil person evil things come from you. When you are a loving person loving things will come from you. Know the difference when it comes to the person you choose marry. Don't be surprised!
Be Blessed!

Marriage Wisdom Moment: Day 137

1 Thessalonians 4:3-5. It is God's will that you should be sanctified: that you should avoid sexual immorality; that each of you should learn to control your own body in a way that is holy and honorable, not in passionate lust like the pagans, who do not know God;

In other words, you should not be in sexual sin like those who don't know God especially if you are married. Remember when you are married you're not only married to your spouse but your also married to God. Don't cheat on God a threefold cord is not easily broken. **Be Blessed!**

Marriage Wisdom Moment: Day 138

1 Corinthians 6:13 You say, "Food for the stomach and the stomach for food, and God will destroy them both." The body, however, is not meant for sexual immorality but for the Lord, and the Lord for the body.

In other words, when you are married you are also married to God especially if you gave your life to him and is having an ongoing relationship with him daily. That's why you shouldn't be out there seeking an affair. God knows your heart and he knows what you are capable of, so if an affair enters your heart ask God to take it away. Remember an affair is thought about before its acted on. **Be Blessed!**

Marriage Wisdom Moment: Day 139

Proverbs 5:18-19 "Let your fountain be blessed, and rejoice in the wife of your youth, a lovely deer, a graceful doe. Let her breasts fill you always with delight; be intoxicated always in her love.

In other words, be satisfied with you own wife's breasts and be infatuated with her love. If we keep our minds on our own spouses we wouldn't be busy looking and being infatuated with someone else's.
Be Blessed!

Marriage Wisdom Moment: Day 140

Genesis 1:28. God blessed them; and God said to them, "Be fruitful and multiply, and fill the earth, and subdue it; and rule over the fish of the sea and over the birds of the sky and over every living thing that moves on the earth.

In other words, God gives us spouses to enjoy sexual intimacy, to be blessed with children when we want them and to rule over the earth. We should be thankful to be blessed with our spouse and not to have to worry about being in sin. Marriage is a blessing, and we should treat it as such. **Be Blessed!**

Marriage Wisdom Moment: Day 141

Titus 1:15. To the pure, all things are pure; but to those who are defiled and unbelieving, nothing is pure, but both their mind and their conscience are defiled.

In other words, make sure the spouse you choose is a believer as you are. The bible says don't be unequally yoked with unbelievers. Don't you know when you marry an unbeliever it makes your marriage much harder. That's why God explained it by saying make sure the one you want to marry is traveling the same road as you otherwise it will be difficult reaching your destination. **Be Blessed!**

Marriage Wisdom Moment: Day 142

Exodus 20:14 - Thou shalt not commit adultery.

In other words, don't go sleeping with anyone else. God did not make marriage for you to defile it by your lustful ways. Once you said I do that means you no longer can with other people. **Be Blessed!**

Marriage Wisdom Moment: Day 143

Song of Solomon 4:10 - How fair is thy love, my sister, [my] spouse! how much better is thy love than wine! and the smell of thine ointments than all spices!

In Other words, be in love with your spouse and be sexually attracted to them in every way. Making love should be so exciting with your spouse. I know sometimes we feel well it's the same person but that's what make marriage unique. When you can enjoy making love over and over to that same person it shows true commitment and stability. **Be Blessed!**

Marriage Wisdom Moment: Day 144

1 Corinthians 7:9. But if they cannot exercise self-control, they should marry. For it is better to marry than to burn with passion.

In other words, as you can see God made marriage, so we can enjoy sex without being in sin. Marriage is a blessing and we should be having lots of sex, love, fun and enjoyment. The singles should be jealous of us because where having so much fun! **Be Blessed!**

Marriage Wisdom Moment: Day 145

Deuteronomy 22:28-29

"If a man meets a virgin who is not betrothed, and seizes her and lies with her, and they are found, then the man who lay with her shall give to the father of the young woman fifty shekels of silver, and she shall be his wife, because he has violated her. He may not divorce her all his days.

In other words, once you get married you should not be seeking to divorce. When God gives you your spouse he looks for you to be faithful and loyal to them. God expects the same thing from us when we give our life to him. Men and women of God should have long lasting true, happy, loyal marriages. **Be Blessed!**

Marriage Wisdom Moment: Day 146

1 Corinthians 6:9
Or do you not know that the unrighteous will not inherit the kingdom of God? Do not be deceived: neither the sexually immoral, nor idolaters, nor adulterers, nor men who practice homosexuality,

In other words, we need to stay in our lane if you are married don't be found in sexual sin when glory comes calling for you because you may not make it in to heaven. Be found faithful, loyal and loving in your marriage. **Be Blessed!**

Marriage Wisdom Moment: Day 147

Genesis 2:25. And the man and his wife were both naked and were not ashamed.

In other words, God made our bodies and as we age things start to gravitate downward, but you should not be ashamed to be naked in front of your spouse. Marriage should be a safe place to be when we feel inadequate about ourselves or we need to vent about something else.
Our spouses should make us feel beautiful about ourselves. Marriage should be a beautiful union with two beautiful people standing together naked and unashamed.
Be Blessed!

Date Night!
Sexual Healing!

Don't you know the marriage bed is undefiled? God made marriage for us to have sex and Lots of sex whenever we can especially on your date night. Where there is a will there is a way. Spice it up explore different positions and different ways you can show your spouse how you love to be with them. Try different lingerie and sexy underwear for him. Try strawberries and cream to spice things up or just try something you always wanted to do with each other this is about your marriage, and it's a no (three-way zone or anything that will defile your marriage bed) kind of love. Love is not selfish, and you should not do anything your spouse is not comfortable with. There is nothing more awesome and vibrant than two people who clearly live to love each other. Let's keep it satisfying.

Date Night Simplified!

1. Sex/Making Love
2. Sexy Lingerie
3. Explore different positions
4. No Defiling the Marriage bed this zone is for two alone.
5.Don't do anything your spouse is not comfortable with.

Why Do We Find Disorder in Marriages?

It's because we apply our own rules to marriage instead of God's rules. When apply wrong rules we reap the bad benefits of those rules but if we apply the right rules we will reap the good results of those rules. The Holy Bible gives us the right keys to unlock the doors in our marriages to being happy and prosperous.

Key# 1-Proper Order

NIV: 1 Corinthians 11:3. But I want you to realize that the head of every man is Christ and the. Head of the woman is a man, and the head of Christ is God.

This is the proper marriage covenant setup. This scripture shows that God and Jesus are one, so the man must submit unto Christ, which is the head of a man, and they must become one, so the woman can be in her place of submission to the man. Submission first starts with the man.

Key#2- Selfishness

NIV: John 3:35. The Father loves the Son and has placed everything in his hands.

Godly love shares their possessions with their spouse we cannot have the attitude that this is mine, and this is yours. Selfishness in any form is NOT of God.

Key # 3- Communication

NIV: John 5:20. For the Father loves the Son and shows him all he does. Yes, and he will show him even greater works than these, so that you will be amazed.

Godly love communicates, both spouses, need to let each other know what they are doing because trust is a major factor in marriage. When we are open with one another, it creates a trust that no devil can stand against it. It's not about trying to control each other it's about our willingness to want our spouses to know what's going on

Key# 4- Honor/ Respect

NIV: "For not even the Father judges anyone, but He has given all judgment to the Son, so that all will honor the Son even as they honor the Father. He who does not honor the Son does not honor the Father, who sent Him.

A loving wife wants her husband to be honored by others. She is willing to share her honor with him she does not belittle him and put him down in front of others thereby dishonoring him. Her husband also sees that he doesn't dishonor her as well.

Key# 5-   Learning your Spouse

NIV: John 10:15. Just as the Father knows me, and I know the Father--and I lay down my life for the sheep.

How well do spouses know each other? Only when they know each other can they grow in love and respect for each other. If married couples want a relationship of true Godly love to succeed, then Christ must be the example that they follow. Christ accepted the father as his head because he knew him. He knew that his father would never abuse his authority over him.

A Marriage will fail if it is based on self-gratification and pleasure only which is the way most marriages are set up in the world today.

WISDOM ON DISAGREEMENTS
CHAPTER 7

Marriage Wisdom Moment: Day 148

1 Peter 3:7. Tells husbands, "Be considerate as you live with your wives, and treat them with respect as the weaker partner and as heirs with you of the gracious gift of life, so that nothing will hinder your prayers."

In other words, the Lord won't listen to your excuses in in trying to say that your wife doesn't act like the weaker vessel or "the reason I act like this is because of the woman you gave me." Nope! The Lord didn't listen to it in the garden at the beginning of time, and He won't accept excuses today for building your house in foolish and unkind ways, no matter what your wife does. Love her any way. **Be Blessed!**

Marriage Wisdom Moment: Day 149

Proverbs 25:28. He that hath no rule over his own spirit is like a city that is broken down without walls.

In other words, you are in control of the way you treat your husband or wife. God is watching how you control your spirit in different situations that occur in marriage. Stop blaming your bad attitude on your husband or wife get control and decide to keep a good spirit. **Be Blessed!**

Marriage Wisdom Moment: Day 150

Proverbs 16:25 say: "There is a way that seems right to a man, but in the end, it leads to death".

In Other words, be careful of "right fighting." Right fighting is fighting to such a degree that you would much rather prove you are right, than to save the relationship. Sometimes you are being so adamant about proving to your spouse that your way is the "right" way, can cause a death in your relationship. Let's be careful God is the only right one. **Be Blessed!**

Marriage Wisdom Moment: Day 151

Proverbs 14:1. Every wise woman builds her house, but the foolish one tears it down with her own hands.

In other words, we as women and wives have the biggest influence in our homes with our kids and in our marriage. We should not be bringing strife jealousy and negativity in our homes and then use it against our family and therefore tearing down our home. Just because your friends are having problems in their home doesn't mean you should bring their problems to your home. Be wise don't bring someone else's situations into your home keep the peace. **Be Blessed!**

Marriage Wisdom Moment: Day 152

Proverbs 15:28. The mind of the righteous studies how to answer, but the mouth of the wicked pours out evil things.

In other words, husbands and wives need to learn how to answer each other in love. At some point in your marriage, you should know the habits of each other to the point of knowing what he or she will say next, once you learn your spouse's ways don't keep flying off the handle. If we love God, we will keep strife down by answering with a loving, answer not argumentative. Learn how to answer in love by studying your partner!
Be Blessed!

Marriage Wisdom Moment: Day 153

Proverbs 16:32. He that is slow to anger is better than the mighty: and he that rule his spirit than he that taketh a city.

In other words, stop blaming your spouse when you lose your temper. You alone are in control of your own spirit. Do you know it takes more strength to not lose control then it does just to go off on someone? Take the blame off your spouse and take responsibility for your own actions. Start learning to control your own spirit if you can't ask God to help you he will. **Be Blessed!**

Marriage Wisdom Moment: Day 154

Proverbs 24:29. Say not, I will do to him what he has done to me: I will repay the man back for his deed.

In other words, don't do wrong to someone who have done wrong to you as payback. Sometimes in marriage we get into disagreements with one another, and that can become heated at times to the point of anger. We just want our spouses to suffer for getting us mad in the first place, but God wants us to take that anger and defuse it by being loving even when you just want to get back at your spouse for what they said or did. Sometimes the hardest thing is to say I'm sorry, but when you show love during anger it will change how you feel about paying them back love conquers all. **Be Blessed!**

Marriage Wisdom Moment: Day 155

Proverbs 23:6. Eat not the bread of him who has a hard grudging and evil eye, neither desire his dainty.

In other words, don't desire to be in the company of those who don't like your husband or wife. Sometimes when we get married we have friends in our lives that don't like our spouses or sometimes there are family members who don't like our spouses. Well, whatever the case you need to cut those toxic people out of your lives, they are jealous and envious, and they will never change. Just change your environment and let God bring you godly friends. Remember your family are those who serve the Lord! **Be Blessed!**

Marriage Wisdom Moment: Day 156

Proverbs 29:22. A man of wrath stirs up strife and a man given to anger commits and causes much transgression.

In other words, are you a man or woman that stir up trouble by what you say? Do you say things to get your spouse or your friends angry causing all kinds of stuff? Then you are an angry person, and you need God's deliverance. Sometimes we are keeping company with people we call our friends that always try to bring us to anger by their words. If you have these toxic people in your life as a married couple pray for them and then release them and allow God to bring you true godly friends to support, you and is positive. If you are an angry spouse, ask God for forgiveness and release the anger and ask God to help you be a more positive person. **Be Blessed!**

Marriage Wisdom Moment: Day 157

2 Timothy 2:23. But refuse foolish and ignorant speculations, knowing that they produce quarrels.

In other words, stop bringing up stupid things to your spouse that will only lead to arguments. We as married couples should learn how to direct our conversations, so they always stay positive not negative. **Be Blessed!**

Marriage Wisdom Moment: Day 158

2 Timothy 2:14. Remind them of these things, and solemnly charge them in the presence of God not to wrangle about words, which is useless and leads to the ruin of the hearers.

In other words, stop speaking useless things that make no sense and can harm those who are listening to it. Don't argue about things that make no sense in front of others or in front of your children especially if profanity is involved. It changes the way people see you both and you're not just hurting others your hurting yourself. **Be Blessed!**

Marriage Wisdom Moment: Day 159

1 Corinthians 6:1 Does any one of you, when he has a case against his neighbor, dare to go to the law before the unrighteous and not before the saints?

In other words, why do you seek advice about your marriage from your worldly friends and family who don't know God instead of seeking advice from your brothers and sister in Christ or your Pastor. Marriage is a God idea, so the world doesn't know how it works. Seek those in a God authority position. **Be Blessed!**

Marriage Wisdom Moment: Day 160

Romans 14:1 Now accept the one who is weak in faith, but not for passing judgment on his opinions.

In other words, people make mistakes so don't be so fast to judge your spouse because they may not know as much about God like you. We need to have a teachable spirit not a judgmental one. **Be Blessed!**

Marriage Wisdom Moment: Day 161

Ephesians 4:31-5:2. Let all bitterness and wrath and anger and clamor and slander be put away from you, along with all malice. Be kind to one another, tenderhearted, forgiving one another, as God in Christ forgave you. Therefore, be imitators of God, as beloved children. And walk in love, as Christ loved us and gave himself up for us, a fragrant offering and sacrifice to God.

In other words, we should walk in love always towards one another. Especially in marriage God wants us to treat each other the way we want to be treated. We need to let all anger and bitterness go especially when someone hurts you in a negative way. Forgiveness is not the removal of your memory ......But the removal of your pain. **Be Blessed!**

Marriage Wisdom Moment: Day 162

Proverbs 17:14. The beginning of strife is like letting out water, so abandon the quarrel before it breaks out.

In other words, husbands learn how to put a fire out before it could even get started. A person can't argue by themselves if we don't get involved in the start of a quarrel we don't have to worry about saying something we don't mean. Learn to stop the quarrel by saying something nice to your spouse it will put the fire out fast. **Be Blessed!**

Marriage Wisdom Moment: Day 163

1 Corinthians 1:11-12. For I have been informed concerning you, my brethren, by Chloe's people, that there are quarrels among you.

In other words, stop fighting so much God didn't allow you to get married to fight all the time. Nobody wants to hear you fighting like cats and dogs, take the time to talk to each other with respect and find out what you're fighting about so much. Learn to listen to each other and do whatever you need to do to get you back to your happy place. **Be Blessed!**

Marriage Wisdom Moment: Day 164

Proverbs 20:3. Keeping away from strife is an honor for a man, but any fool will quarrel.

In other words, if you are wise you will stay away from trouble especially when you see it coming in your marriage. Only a fool wants to fight and argue all time over nothing. Take your spouse to prayer if they are the fool. Only God can make them wise. **Be Blessed!**

Marriage Wisdom Moment: Day 165

Proverbs 26:17. Like one who takes a dog by the ears Is he who passes by and meddles with strife not belonging to him.

In other words, keep people out of your marital business who cannot help you with any of your problems. Telling someone your business who can't help you is like asking single person for marriage advice. Watch who meddles in your marriage with your permission. **Be Blessed!**

Marriage Wisdom Moment: Day 166

1 Corinthians 3:3-4. for you are still fleshly. For since there is jealousy and strife among you, are you not fleshly, and are you not walking like mere men?

In other words, stop walking in your flesh by acting jealous and angry. God don't want you acting like that towards your spouse. Learn how to trust God over your marriage and your spouse. Only God can change your life and situation. **Be Blessed!**

Marriage Wisdom Moment: Day 167

Romans 14:19. So then we pursue the things which make for peace and the building up of one another.

In other words, let's build each other up in positivity and not in negativity. We as married couples are supposed to help each other become better. Remember iron sharpens iron so when we help each other we become better. **Be Blessed!**

Marriage Wisdom Moment: Day 168

Romans 16:17. Now I urge you, brethren, keep your eye on those who cause dissensions and hindrances contrary to the teaching which you learned, and turn away from them.

In other words, watch people who try to cause trouble in your marriage. It could be friends, family or in-laws just keep your eye on your marriage. Don't let others give their negative opinion about your spouse. I don't care what you are going through. When we let other's opinions of our spouse come in we began to see our spouses through their eyes instead of God's eyes.

Be Blessed!

Date Night!
Cooking Together!

Why not cook for each other tonight? You could both make each other's favorite dish together and enjoy it on those best dishes you only save for special guest. Why not make dinner like you would have it in a restaurant like steamed crab legs and salad or grilled steaks if the weather permits. Try spaghetti and garlic bread you, know just be creative and laugh and enjoy each other while the food is cooking. Make sure your alone get a sitter so you can. Stay home and have this beautiful romantic dinner. Rent some romantic movies and make some popcorn in a popcorn bucket, so your hands meet in the bucket. Just make it fun and sexy!

Date Night Simplified!

1.Get a sitter if you have kids/or put the kids to bed early
2. Make each other's favorite dish together
3. Use those special dishes you only use for special guest
4. Rent some romantic movies or action-packed and watch them while eating popcorn from the same bowl
5. Make it fun and sexy

Thomas & Patricia's Story

Pastor Thomas and I met in the year of 1991 at a friend of mine and a niece of his house warming party. We were introduced to each other at a casual meet and greet portion of the party, and we thought no more of it afterwards. One afternoon in the spring of two thousand my friend called me and asked me if I remembered her uncle. She introduced me to him at her house warming party nine years earlier and I said yes, but I had not thought of him since then. She told me he asked about me after nine years.

I told her I was waiting on God to send the right man into my life. The bible says when a man finds a wife… Her immediate response was "I believe this is God" then she invited me out with her and her husband and her uncle on a double date, and I accepted the invitation. After that night, we began to call one another on the phone after about a month of that I was invited to a revival at his church I attended, and I did enjoy myself. We went on several more dates all during the day time as to not make provisions for the flesh to sin.

Our first date night was spent on the lakefront in downtown Sanford FL in the car watching the ducks and listening to CeCe Winans cd Alabaster Box oh how I love that cd to this day. In the month of August, we talked about marriage not knowing or realizing that God was at work. On September eighteenth, two thousand, we were married. Our courtship only lasted four months and as of September eighteenth, two thousand and fourteen we will be celebrating fourteen years of marriage.

The marriage was ordained and anointed by God to last a lifetime. We were called to minister as a couple to the Kingdom for such a time as this. We learned a valuable lesson to keep Christ as the center of our marriage. If we tried to love each other on our own, it would be impossible.

The least little thing we do to annoy or raise one another's temper would cause us to see each other as the object of our love, but through Christ and from Christ flow the agape (love unconditional) kind of love. There is nothing we can do to disturb it. Our secret for a successful, happy and prosperous marriage is to follow God's plan. We have challenges, but we can work through them. The bible says love never fails. It's the love of and a love for Christ that keeps our marriage strong.

WISDOM ON FAMILY
CHAPTER 8

MARRIAGE WISDOM MOMENT: DAY 169

Proverbs 23:24. The father of the righteous will greatly rejoice; he who fathers a wise son will be glad in him."

In other words, we all want to raise wise children, but parents need to understand that children will mostly learn from what they see at home. If you want wise children teach them wise things and it will show. **Be Blessed!**

Marriage Wisdom Moment: Day 170

Psalm 217:1. "Lo, children are a heritage of the LORD: and the fruit of the womb is his reward."

In other words, children are a blessing from God and a reward so let's be a great example of how we expect them to be when they are older. You can't want something for your child you're not willing to do or are not already doing or encouraging them to do.
Be Blessed!

Marriage Wisdom Moment: Day 171

Colossians 3:20 says: Children, obey your parents in everything, for this pleases the Lord.

In other words, if you have a child that disrespects you then they do not please the Lord, and you need to correct that behavior, or you need to take them to God in prayer. Sometimes children learn to disrespect their mother because they see their father doing it. Or you see them disrespecting their father because they see their mother doing it either way parents let's not do those things in front of our child it does change the way they think about respect. **Be Blessed!**

Marriage Wisdom Moment: Day 172

Ephesians 6:1. Children, obey your parents in the Lord, for this is right. "Honor your father and mother," which is the first commandment with promise: "that it may be well with you, and you may live long on the earth."

In other words, Children are to do what their parents say. It bothers me when I see these modern-day parents ruining the futures of their children because they do not give them discipline. These modern-day children are doing whatever they want and living lawless lives and I can tell you they will not be successful unless these parents get a hold of them. If you don't know, God get to know him and his word now! So, you can execute God's plan on how to raise your children. **Be Blessed!**

Marriage Wisdom Moment: Day 173

Matthew 19:14. Jesus said, "Let the little children come to me, and do not hinder them, for the kingdom of heaven belongs to such as these."

In other words, we as parents are not to hinder our children from knowing who God is and what he has done for them. We as parents sometimes don't want to go to church and therefore we hinder the children if they want to go. We as parents should be raising our children up in the fear of the Lord especially because this world is hard enough to live in without him. Let's encourage our children to come to Jesus. **Be Blessed!**

Marriage Wisdom Moment: Day 174

Proverbs 20:11. Even a child is known by his actions, by whether his conduct is pure and right.

In other words, people can tell if your children are being raised right by their actions and their conduct. If your child is cursing, you out then he or she is not being raised right. If they are talking back to you, they are not being raised right. Your children wouldn't be doing those things if the parents were parenting and not trying to be your kid's friends. If you don't know how to be a parent, then read your bible it will tell you how. **Be Blessed!**

Marriage Wisdom Moment: Day 175

Proverbs 23:24-26. The father of a righteous man has great joy; he who has a wise son delight in him. May your father and mother be glad; may she who gave you birth rejoice! My son, give me your heart and let your eyes keep to my ways,

In other words, our children should be brought up in the ways of God and that way they will keep his ways once they become older. Sometimes we grow up in an environment that wasn't of God but at some point, when we become adults we should be looking into our own traditions of how we should bring our kids up. If we were raised in an abusive home, we should not want to repeat that same abuse in the lives of our own children. We need to look to God to help us raise our children the way he directs us to. Raise them in the fear of God and with respect. **Be Blessed!**

Marriage Wisdom Moment: Day 176

Proverbs 25:22 Listen to your father, who gave you life, and do not despise your mother when she is old.

In other words, listen to your parents especially if they are giving you some wisdom about life. They have lived longer than you, and they should know what they are saying. I know we all don't get honorable parents, but we are to honor them. God gave you the parents you have and if they are not giving you any wisdom on life ask God to give it to you. God will help you when your mother and father can't. **Be Blessed!**

Marriage Wisdom Moment: Day 177

Proverbs 4:1 Listen, my sons, to a father's instruction; pay attention and gain understanding.

In other words, when we listen we gain more knowledge. Some children are hot headed and don't want to listen to no one, but when they do that they are nothing but fools. When you don't want wisdom then, you will follow everything presented to you but if you have knowledge and wisdom, the enemy won't be able to lead you in the wrong direction. Learning, listening and using wisdom is the key. **Be Blessed!**

Marriage Wisdom Moment: Day 178

Proverbs 6:20 says: My son, keep your father's commands and do not forsake your mother's teaching.

In other words, don't go asking for advice you know you're not going to listen to. Adult children are always asking their parents for advice and then still go do the opposite of what was said. Why waste time asking for advice just go and do what you already had in mine. Pray about the situation first and then if you don't want anyone's' advice just keep it between you and God.
Be Blessed!

Marriage Wisdom Moment: Day 179

Proverbs 8:32-33 says: Now then, my sons, listen to me; blessed are those who keep my ways. Listen to my instruction and be wise; do not ignore it.

In other words, God has given us instructions on how to live and how to pray, so why are you always going through rough times? It sounds like you are not reading your bible or talking it over in prayer to God. Trouble don't last always so if you are always struggling you need to get into your word and get some wisdom and talk this thing out with God. Only he can help you change your situation. **Be Blessed!**

Marriage Wisdom Moment: Day 180

Proverbs 10:1 says: A wise son brings joy to his father, but a foolish son grief to his mother.

In other words, do what you were taught especially if you were taught love and respect. Why is it that you teach your children to do the right thing, but when they are challenged with peer pressure they don't show what they know? Stop trying to fit in where you don't. God made you different, and he set you aside to be used for his glory. A lot of times when we are struggling through life it's because God wants us to ask him for help and then he wants us not to hide the fact that he is helping us. Stop being foolish trying to fit in and if God has called you let the world know. Don't be ashamed of him who has saved you. **Be Blessed!**

Marriage Wisdom Moment: Day 181

Proverbs 13:1. "A wise child accepts a parent's discipline; a mocker refuses to listen to correction."

In other words, a wise child will listen to instructions and do them and when they are corrected they will accept it. Only a disobedient child will mock what is being spoken and re-bel. Keep your children before the Lord! **Be Blessed!**

Marriage Wisdom Moment: Day 182

Deuteronomy 6:6-7. These commandments that I give you today are to be on your hearts. Impress them on your children. Talk about them when you sit at home and when you walk along the road, when you lie down and when you get up.

In other words, talk to your children about the Lord and show them the things of the Lord. Let you children know it's hard living without God in their lives let them know they need him every step of the way to guide them along in life.

Be Blessed!

Marriage Wisdom Moment: Day 183

Acts 16:31. They replied, "Believe in the Lord Jesus, and you will be saved—you and your household."

In other words, when we believe God our whole households are saved and blessed. Let's teach our families about Jesus we need him to light our paths.
Be Blessed!

Marriage Wisdom Moment: Day 184

1 Corinthians 1:10. I appeal to you, brothers and sisters, in the name of our Lord Jesus Christ, that all of you agree with one another in what you say and that there be no divisions among you, but that you be perfectly united in mind and thought.

In other words, in our families we should be on one accord with the way the family is going. As far as me and my house we will serve the Lord. We need to train up our children to know God and learn of his ways. Our children should be saved but they should understand God and make that decision on their own to get saved and serve him and we as parents should be in agreement with that decision.

Be Blessed!

Marriage Wisdom Moment: Day 185

1 John 4:20. Whoever claims to love God yet hates a brother or sister is a liar. For whoever does not love their brother and sister, whom they have seen, cannot love God, whom they have not seen.

In other words, we can not say we love God and hate our own family members. We need to understand that even if our family members don't serve God he still created them, and he will deal with them accordingly. Love them anyway even in their sin. **Be Blessed!**

Marriage Wisdom Moment: Day 186

Psalm 133:1. How good and pleasant it is when God's people live together in unity!

In other words, God want us to live with each other in peace and he wants us to enjoy life and each other as family. Family time should be important in marriage we should not always put our jobs and other things before our family time. If you are working super hard you should play super hard. Enjoy your family and have fun.
Be Blessed!

Marriage Wisdom Moment: Day 187

Ephesians 6:4. Fathers, do not exasperate your children; instead, bring them up in the training and instruction of the Lord.

In other words, husbands let's teach our children what they need to know about God. Teach them the word of God and how to live their lives in the ways of God walking the path he already set before them.
Be Blessed!

Marriage Wisdom Moment: Day 188

Proverbs 22:6. Start children off on the way they should go, and even when they are old they will not turn from it.

In other words, let's teach our children the right things and the right way to live and they will remember it when they get older. The word of God is the most important word to teach them. When we live and love in the Lord our children will never forget it. **Be Blessed!**

Marriage Wisdom Moments: Day 189

Joshua 24:15. But if serving the Lord seems undesirable to you, then choose for yourselves this day whom you will serve, whether the gods your ancestors served beyond the Euphrates, or the gods of the Amorites, in whose land you are living. But as for me and my household, we will serve the Lord.

In other words, choose as a family who you will serve. God wants us to know him, love him and follow his ways. When we do that we protect our family from whatever the enemy might have in store for them. Serving the Lord as a family is the best thing you can do. Keep your family before God in prayer. **Be Blessed!**

Marriage Wisdom Moment: Day 190

1 Timothy 5:8. Anyone who does not provide for their relatives, and especially for their own household, has denied the faith and is worse than an unbeliever.

In other words, when you don't provide financially, spiritually and mentally for your own family you are looked at like someone who don't even know God. If we are children of God, we should be providing for our families the way God intended. God gives us finances to defend our selves against the mortgage/rent, the electric bill and the water bill so we need to use what he gave us to take care of our family.
Be Blessed!

Date Night!
It's My Night!

Ok, it's the other spouses turn to have a night about them only. If it's the wife's night, then husbands let's do something she really would enjoy. Don't you know there is nothing sexier than a man cleaning the house, cooking, dinner, doing the laundry and arranging for some quality time with your wife. There is nothing sexier than for the scene to be set for whatever you want to do. Ok wives set the scene for your husband if it's his turn do something he likes and go all the way out for him let him know you have his back and all his other sides. Take care of whatever he wants. Let your heart be your guide.

Date Night Simplified!

1. Make it all about the other person
2. Set the scene
3. Make the evening ready for your spouse
4. Have your game face on be ready
5. Do whatever comes to mind just let your heart guide you

Keys of the Kingdom for a Happy Marriage

Marriages today need repair because marriage is not taken as a serious covenant made before God and man. We're not seeing a lot of successful marriages today because people have their own ideas about marriage and how to do marriage instead of seeing what the bible says will keep your marriage. Couples who desire to keep your marriage and who want to stay married must realize that God himself made marriage and so to know about marriage we should be seeking his way of doing it. No matter what your religion is or what you're presently going through if you begin to get into the word of God and follow his keys to marriage you will have a happy and successful marriage.

Kingdom Keys:

1# God must be the head of your marriage for a marriage to be happy and successful for life. The husband and wife must include God as a partner in their marriage, and together they both yield to what God instructs in the word about marriage.

2# Wives are to be submissive to your own husband in everything.

3# Husbands are to love your wife as Christ love the church and his own body.

4# Man shall leave his family and cleave to his wife

.

5# the wife is to respect and reverence her husband.

Remember these are keys to having a happy and lasting marriage

Prayer OF Salvation

Do You Know Where Your Soul Will Go When You Leave This Earth? **Revelation 3 vs 20 says: Behold I stand at the door and knock. If anyone hears my voice and opens the door, I will come into him and dine with him and he with me.**

Now repeat this prayer: Dear Lord Jesus I believe you died for me and rose on the third day. I confess that I am a sinner. Please come into my heart and forgive my sins. I need your love, and I need you to save me. I receive eternal life. Confirm your love by giving me peace, joy and love for those that hurt me Amen. You are now Saved!

Marriage Prayer

Dear Heavenly Father I thank you for the mate you specifically designed just for me. I understand that marriage is a covenant, and I am to take my vows seriously just as I take giving my life to you seriously. Forgive me for the times I took my wife/husband for granted and all that you have blessed me with. I speak these words before you from my heart. I now take my covenant vows before you God and the Holy Spirit seriously. I will no longer take my wife/husband and family for granted.

I will appreciate what you have given me, and I will follow your direction in this marriage because you made marriage, and I don't know the total direction you want this marriage to go. Help me to show my spouse the love that you desire and help us to respect and honor one another the way your word tells us to. I love you, and I desire that you be the head of this marriage guiding us every step of the way until Glory comes. Thank you, Lord, and I know that this prayer is now answered In Jesus name Amen.

ABOUT THE AUTHOR

Loretta Pittman has been married to her handsome husband for thirty years, and they have been in ministry for over thirteen years. They have four grown children and four grandchildren. I have been a born-again believer since 1995 when I rededicated my life to Christ.

My belief is that Jesus is the son of God and only through him can you be saved. Loretta and William are the founders of New Covenant of Faith Int'l Ministries and Marriage Café, which is a Facebook based community forum that helps struggling marriages.

This book was birthed out of my pain in struggling to become a submissive wife and, my pain in becoming one with my husband. I have a Master's in Christian Counseling and a Bachelors in Christian Education.

Copyright@2014 Scriptures Publishing

No Part of this book may be reproduced or used in any
form or by any means, graphic, electronic or mechanical,
including photo copying, recording, taping, and
information retrieval systems, without the prior written
permission of Scriptures Publishing

All Scripture was found In the King James Bible and
the NIV. Bible

If you would like Prayer for your marriage, please leave
your Prayer Request at www.dailymarriagewisdom.com.
Or In box us and follow us on Facebook at
www.facebook.com/MarriageCaFe1.

Do you struggle with drugs and alcohol?
Are you struggling with Sexual sin?
Are you dealing with your children being taken away
from you?

If you are then this book is a Must Read!!!!!!!

Go get your Copy Today!!!!!! @ Amazon

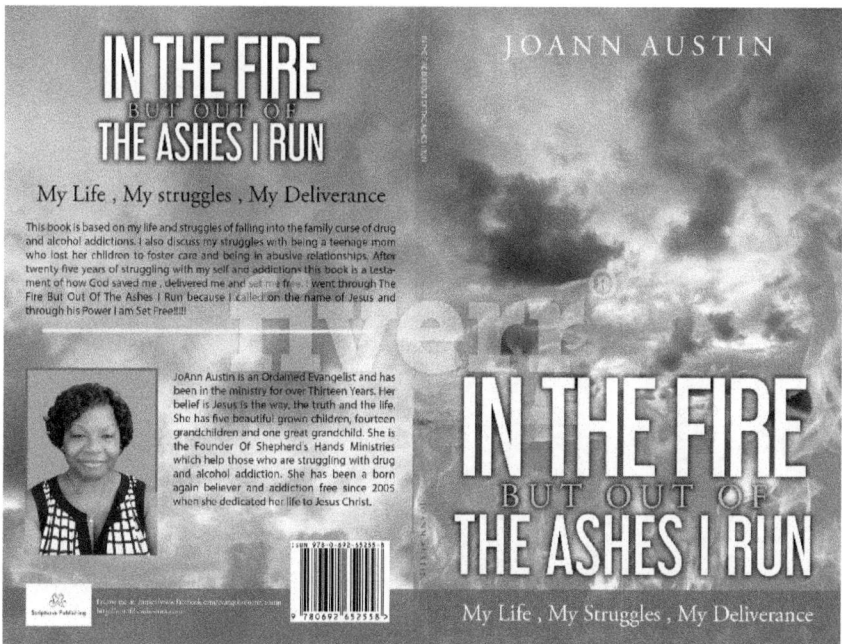

Notes

Notes:

Notes:

Notes:

Notes:

Notes:

www.ingramcontent.com/pod-product-compliance
Lightning Source LLC
LaVergne TN
LVHW051041080426
835508LV00019B/1641